THE COLLECTION
MOMENTS OF FINDING GOD RIGHT WHERE WE ARE

The Collection: Moments of Finding God Right Where We Are
Copyright © 2024 by Rhonda J. Kane

Published in the United States of America

Library of Congress Control Number: 2024916532
ISBN   Paperback: 979-8-89091-677-8
ISBN   eBook: 979-8-89091-678-5

All rights reserved. No part of this publication may be reproduced, stored in a retrieval system or transmitted in any way by any means, electronic, mechanical, photocopy, recording or otherwise without the prior permission of the author except as provided by USA copyright law.

The opinions expressed by the author are not necessarily those of ReadersMagnet, LLC.

ReadersMagnet, LLC
10620 Treena Street, Suite 230 | San Diego, California, 92131 USA
1.619. 354. 2643 | www.readersmagnet.com

Book design copyright © 2024 by ReadersMagnet, LLC. All rights reserved.

Cover Image by Rhonda J. Kane
Cover design by Jhiee Oraiz
Interior design by Don De Guzman

THE COLLECTION

MOMENTS OF FINDING GOD RIGHT WHERE WE ARE

RHONDA J. KANE

Contents

Foreword ix

Chapter 1: Mercy 1
    Time Out 2
    Singing Over Me 4
    You Are Dismissed 7
    Simply Mercy 10
    My Screen Protector 13
    Breaking Laws 16
    What's That Smell? 20
    Asking For Help 23
    Blessed Are Those 26
    It's Called Mercy 28

Chapter 2: Family 31
    Time Travel 32
    The Wedding 37
    A Grandmother's Prayer 40
    Dearest Daughter 42
    The One About My Amazing Dad 44
    Sixteen with Dreams 46
    Ketchup 50
    Father's Day Date 52
    1 Corinthians 13 54

Chapter 3: Just Jesus 56
    Humility On a Donkey 57
    He Is Worthy 60
    Good Friday 62

    The Man on the Middle Cross 65
    Beyond the Veil 68
    Rejecting Rejection 71
    Only You 74
    It's Saturday 76
    Forgiven Much Loves Much 78
    It's Easter Morning 80

Chapter 4: Lessons 82
    Lessons 82
    Auschwitz 83
    The Simplest Lesson 86
    Picking Up the Pieces 89
    Lose the Baggage 91
    Be An Enabler 94
    Replacing Worry With a Chef 97
    Distractions 99
    The Girl On the Top Bunk 101
    Nowhere Else But the Heart 103

Chapter 5: Friends 105
    It Looks Like Jesus 106
    Some Beauty Never Fades 109
    Praying For My Friend 112
    Losing My Friend 114
    Saying Good-bye 117
    His Church 119
    Raymond 123
    The Table 126
    Grandma's Path 128

Chapter 6: Be Intentional 130
    Use Your Words 131
    Still Standing 133
    My Wagon 135
    Choices 138
    The Day 140

 Love Yourself As Your Neighbor 142
 Missed Opportunities..145
 The Club 148
 My Peace 151
 Regrets and Ribs..153

Chapter 7: Trust 156
 My Requests.His Answers...157
 Two Coins..160
 Great Is Thy Faithfulness...162
 Radical 164
 How Things Used To Be 167
 It's All I Have. It's Everything I Have......................................169
 It's Just Emotion...172
 Lord, Please Make It Enough 175
 Running With Focus..177
 Giants Fall Hard..179
 Looking For the Miracle..181

Chapter 8: Mom 183
 Kindness Lives On 184
 Faithfulness 186
 Waiting and Trusting..189
 His Visit 191
 One Last Lesson From Mom 194
 Mom's Last Goodbye..195
 Heaven 198
 Transitions 201
 Enjoy The Best Mother's Day 203
 Mom's Durango 204

Chapter 9: Inspired 206
 Sunglasses and Transistors..207
 Never Too Late to Shine 210
 Marlene 213
 Live Love 215
 Thoughts of an Old Testament Journey................................218

The Shop Rag 220
Stand Up 222
Just What I Needed...224
What a Difference Thirty-three Years Made.........................227
Be A Beverly..230

Chapter 10: Let's Get Real..232
Coffee and Dad..233
Our Victor is Coming! 235
Camp Kane...237
The God Shed..239
Handing Out Starbucks 241
The Most Important One 243
Graduation Consolation...246
The Woman at the Grocery Store...................................248
The First Three 252
What Exactly Is Normal?..254

Notes 257

Closing Reflections...259

Foreword

Never in a million years would I have thought someone would ask me to write a foreword for their book.

With that said, never in a million years would I have thought I would be married to an author!

Maybe I'm a little prejudiced when it comes to this author, and I probably am since she's my best friend and my wife. So much for the disclaimer.

This gives me a unique insight when it comes to this author and this book. I know Rhonda better than anyone on earth. She's my soulmate. I can tell you she is the real deal. I've never known anyone who hears God's voice clearer than Rhonda. She is adept at taking the most ordinary events and revealing what God is trying to tell us by letting Him speak through her writing.

Rhonda's writing comes from her heart, and she has a wonderful heart.

Like all of us, she has insecurities, but she also has great courage to push past those insecurities and put them on the page because she knows God wants her to.

I hope that after you read this book, it will inspire you to examine your own life and reveal what God is trying to tell you, too.

Dean Kane

Chapter 1

Mercy

Mercy.
I'm good at throwing around the word.
I have used it lightly.
I have felt its weightiness bring me to my knees.
It is fitting that we start here.

Mercy is the compassionate treatment of those in distress, especially when it is within one's power to punish or harm them.

We've all been at the point of giving mercy. But even more so, we have all received mercy. I have never been at the receiving end of mercy when I truly deserved it. That's usually my first frustration when I must give it to others. They don't deserve it.
I need to rethink.

Jesus said it best:

> *"Blessed are the merciful, for they will be shown mercy." --Matthew 5:7 NIV*

Go and do likewise.

Time Out

*We all reach moments when we are found in our figurative desert. This particular piece found me there. Great words of advice had come years ago from a wonderful pastor and friend, "Don't waste your wilderness." I have never forgotten those words.

Have you ever watered a neglected flower bed amidst a dry, hot summer and thought you would never get it saturated? The life-giving water filled every crevice and soaked into the parched, dry soil. The flowers didn't revive immediately but took their time returning to life and vibrancy. Sometimes, they needed several days and extra watering as well. Have you ever felt like one of those flowers? It has been a long season, for sure. Admittedly, I have a strong resemblance right now to a wilting, scorched sunflower. I have continued to water faithfully, going to the source of all life, but possibly I haven't let it sink in. The elements around me have played havoc as well. They have left me weather-worn, drooping, weary, and unable to give what others might need. Recognizing that, I stop. It feels good.

I have fallen into a peace that it's okay not to be okay. It's okay to sit for a spell before continuing down the road. There have been many things. Some have arrived in a restless world packed with confused, angry people. Some have presented as family illnesses and dissension. Some are nothing but politics and people who need something to disagree about. The loss of a friend I valued dearly could be the straw that broke the back. So. Here I sit. Quietly. The Book is open in front of me. Never has there been so much wisdom, comfort, and peace from His Words. There is no hurry to return to the path, just time to allow Him to restore and help me become all He expects me to be, not what I hope to be.

It is time to lay down demands that I place on myself to be more than I can ever possibly be. It's time to stop worrying about whether I have met anyone else's bar.
It's just time to sit and allow myself to be replenished.
And in the quiet is everything I need.

He hears before I even speak.
He comforts before I even reach.
He loves before I ever cry out.
He gives strength before I even realize how weak I am.
And so I will sit until He fills me.
I will be still until I am saturated and vibrant once again.
He blesses so that I might, in turn, bless others.

And He will restore. He does every time.
My job is to stop long enough to allow Him.
I am allowing Him.

> *"As the deer pants for streams of water, so my soul pants for you, my God. My soul thirsts for God, for the living God. When can I go and meet with God?" --Psalms 42:1-2 NIV*

Lord,
I know where I can meet with you. I will find you wherever I seek you. I enjoy the quiet of the morning as we sit together, looking at your words, longing to understand them, and praying to grow in your spirit. Amen.

Singing Over Me

Fidgety and restless, she just couldn't get her body to slow down. I motion to her, and she climbs onto my lap. I begin to rock. I know that she is three, probably past the rocking age, according to some doctor somewhere. She needs rest, so I am indifferent to any opinion.
"Sing that song to me, Gramma."
I start the melody and sing, "Hush little baby, don't say a word…"

My sweet and thoughtful granddaughter sings softly with me but only makes it to the part about the dog named Rover. My life hits pause momentarily as I soak up the warmth and joy that only a sleeping grandchild can give. After laying her down on the couch and staring at her long eyelashes, I pulled out my Bible to finish today's study. It's been a journey as I've made my way through the Old Testament. I haven't just read; I've studied. I've bought maps and guides, read different versions, read footnotes, and studied commentaries. The message has been prevalent throughout.

God promises.
He provides.
We are stubborn.
He warns. We make wrong choices. Sometimes we are punished.
He forgives and redeems.
Always faithful, He forgives and redeems.
The path for Jesus is forged.

I am beginning to think I have a pretty clear picture of God's nature, but today, I am stopped in my tracks. Finishing the book of Zephaniah, the minor prophet, I read the last section, the promise of the final restoration. I read the words from chapter three, verse 17, and I read again.

> *"The Lord your God is with you, the Mighty Warrior who saves. He will take great delight in you; in his love he will no longer rebuke you, but will rejoice over you with singing." --Zephaniah 3:17 NIV*

Wait! What? I've read this before. I've heard this before, but today, it resonates so deeply. My God, the creator of the universe, the all-powerful and mighty God, is singing over me? As I picture what I just encountered with my granddaughter, the warmth of my Creator envelopes me. Tenderness, gentleness, affection, security. I knew He possessed these qualities, but at this moment, it's personal.

He fights for me, and not only that, He saves me.
He rejoices over me with gladness. Me? Yes, me.
He will be quiet in His love, not dredging up my past ugly sins.
He will delight in me with singing.

As I am held in that scripture and His love, I try to picture God singing over me. I close my eyes. I concentrate. I cannot imagine it, no matter how hard I try.
But I can feel it.
I can sense it.
It is peace.
It is calm.
It is joy.
It is amazing.
And today, it is just what I need.
I cannot explain that kind of love.
I don't have to.
I'll just rest in it.
And who doesn't need rest?

> *"He brought me out into a spacious place; he rescued me because he delighted in me." --Psalms 18:19 NIV*

Lord, My heart leaps for joy at the thought of you finding delight in me and singing over me. Hush my heart as I argue, "But, wait." I am so grateful that you love me this much. Today, may I just rest in that. Amen.

You Are Dismissed

You are dismissed.
Those were grand words to hear in school, college, a long meeting, a lengthy training, and even a long church service. But they are devastating words when we receive them from another human being. Most of the time, we don't hear the words; we feel them. You might be ghosted or deflected when you reach out. You are not chosen. You may find yourself sitting at the sideline of a peer group and feeling overlooked, not included.

In my experience, those words, "You are dismissed," were pointed in my direction. But were they? Perceptions are our reality, and there are times that I have felt dismissed, dismissed from friends, co-workers, family members, and ultimately church members. There's probably not a more confusing, desolate spot than to be left on the edge wondering. It's a lonely corner when you're pondering why you don't fit, why you've been omitted, and the impression that you do not measure up.

In my quest to understand this, I first and foremost realized that my affirmation needs to come from God and God alone, my creator. But as any human, I struggle with this. I want to fit in; I long to be included. I desire to be accepted; I want to be loved. No one wants to feel like they are on the outside looking in. For me, it's not so much as if I'm missing a party, but maybe I'm missing a chance to reach out to someone, help someone, love someone, and be a part of an inclusive group. I've struggled with this a lot in my lifetime, and could it be that most of my struggle has come from miscommunication or misperception? But is it perceivable to think that the entirety has come from that?

So, what is there for me to learn from this?

#1 I regress; God is the one that I must seek affirmation from. His book makes that very clear. He has chosen me.

> *"You did not choose me, but I chose you and appointed you so that you might go and bear fruit—fruit that will last—and so that whatever you ask in my name, the Father will give you." --John 15: 16 NIV*

#2 Have I said or done things that have offset people? It's imperative to check yourself occasionally.

> *"Do not let any unwholesome talk come out of your mouths, but only what is helpful for building others up according to their needs, that it may benefit those who listen." --Ephesians 4:29 NIV*

#3 Have I unintentionally presented arrogance in my conversations, motives, and reactions?
Are there people in my life tha*t I* have dismissed?

> *"Do nothing out of selfish ambition or vain conceit. Rather, in humility value others above yourselves," --Philippians 2:3 NIV*

The latter is the one I want to explore the most.
Who have I left with the impression I didn't need in my circle?
We all need each other.
We all need acceptance, love, and inclusion. We must ensure we give that to others to expect it to return to us.

It all lands on the prayer of Saint Frances of Assisi. Focusing outward, we will be filled inward:

Lord, make me an instrument of your peace:
where there is hatred, let me sow love;
where there is injury, pardon;
where there is doubt, faith;
where there is despair, hope;

where there is darkness, light;
where there is sadness, joy.
O divine Master, grant that I may not so much seek
to be consoled as to console,
to be understood as to understand,
to be loved as to love.
For it is in giving that we receive,
it is in pardoning that we are pardoned,
and it is in dying that we are born to eternal life. Amen

Simply Mercy

Bar the door, I'm about to get honest. I have been studying rejection lately. According to The Cambridge Dictionary, to reject something is to refuse to accept, use, or believe something or someone, to not give someone the love and attention they want and are expecting from you. 1
My definition goes a lot deeper than that. Injustices, disagreements, passive-aggressive statements made toward me in the past; you might say I have collected all of these in a jar and labeled them "Rhonda's rejection."

Reading through Mark 3 this morning, I watched Jesus heal a man's hand out of compassion. It was on the Sabbath. He is quickly rejected, and a plan is birthed to kill him. Again, in John 18, Jesus faces opposition and strong rejection after his arrest—rejection to the point of being struck.

His response?
He spoke truth.
He was matter-of-fact.
He did not become argumentative, defensive, or combative.
After receiving a blow to his face, he merely inquired, "Why did you strike me"?

Unfortunately, I admit this resembles nothing of how I respond when I have been handed injustice, when I feel someone has insinuated things toward me, when I feel left out, or when I feel an inadequacy imposed on me by man's scales.
Nope. I revisit the headstone of that sacred wound often.
I stomp around on it to see if it's gone. My obsession only adds to the injury and increases the pain.

I have to tell others about it so they are aware of my pain. You know, so that they can pray for me.

I tell others. You know, so I can protect them so they are not hurt by the "victimizer."

I tell others because I want to spew what has now become my resentment. There's the keyword: my resentment.

Not once did I witness Jesus carrying resentment in the Scriptures. Not once did I see him having to tell somebody else so they would pray or they would be made aware of his pain. The unjust exchange, rejection, or whatever occurred between Jesus and the person may have had an audience, but Jesus didn't create it.

No need to bring attention to it.

No need to nurse the wound.
No need to keep inflicting pain.

I've been nursing past pain with the wrong medicine.

I want to be like Jesus, but I realize I have a lot of practice ahead of me.
I have to learn to let things go.
I have to allow Him to be my focus.

> *"You will keep in perfect peace those whose minds are steadfast because they trust in you. Trust in the Lord forever, for the Lord, the Lord himself, is the Rock eternal." --Isaiah 26:3-4 NIV*

The bottom line is I am God's child.
I am called to model my Creator and my Redeemer.
I am his daughter, and I am called to live and look like Him. I must be anchored to Him, tethered to Him, focused on Him.

I have been given mercy—probably in amounts more considerable than most.
I identify with the Apostle Paul:

"Christ Jesus came into the world to save sinners—of whom I am the worst." --1 Timothy 1:15 NIV

Today, I will take this reminder with me.
Throughout my life, I have handed out rejection, injustice, and passive-aggressive words.
And in return, God handed out to me--mercy.
May I resemble my Creator.
May my response be simply mercy.

Lord, Help me live this. Amen.

My Screen Protector

I carefully peeled off the plastic wrapper and placed the screen protector on my phone. There, that ought to do it. The guarantee on the box said it would provide adequate protection for the glass on my screen. Yep, they were right. Numerous times, my hands had haphazardly tossed the phone across the room. It remained unscathed.

I began to think about the flip side.

There were ways the screen had protected me. In all reality, it had the potential to be a shield I could hide behind. Possibly, our screens have become that for all of us to some extent.

Hear me out with a few minuscule examples.

My screen allows me to present myself on social media however I want to be perceived. I'm not one to air my dirty laundry on Facebook or Instagram regarding hurt feelings or marital disputes, but I would post a beautiful sunrise instead. I certainly don't want you to see anger in my heart when I'm mad at my husband, neighbor, or family.

The screen allows me to passive-aggressively toss out "thoughts" if I desire, followed by the disclaimer, "Not here to argue…I'll delete if you do."

The screen also protects me when I'm texting. I am safe as long as I carefully send the correct text to the intended person.

I have, on occasion, botched that one up. 😐

The biggie that stood out today is that the screen has helped me become all too complacent with our free store ministry at the Orange Swan.

I'm going to take down the shield for a moment. Here's the real story.

My job, family, and life only allow me time to field some calls for the Orange Swan. In a fantasy world, a full-time secretary would be lovely. So, to process messages, requests, and donations, inquiries are handled primarily through text. Right or wrong, the screen gives me the privilege to distance myself. The screen allows the person to become just a "request." In this ministry's longevity of 11 years, it has become too easy to forget Matthew 25. It's too easy to forget that when I'm helping someone out, I'm doing it for Jesus.

Today was a reminder of that fact.

Someone messaged me several days ago about a need. My schedule did not allow me to take care of it, and to be honest, I hadn't given it much thought, let alone prayed about it.

My schedule cleared a bit, allowing me time to shop for a few groceries for this family and get them some gas. I stood facing them at the fuel pump and looked them in the eye.

They were real.

There wasn't a screen between us to protect me. My heart saw two struggling parents. They were at a point in their life where finances were stressed. Their voices were grateful, their baby smiled happily, and I wondered why I hadn't cleared my schedule days ago or called outside help to minister to this family.

I argued that it was all because of the screen protector. I had allowed it to protect me from seeing the person and feeling their pain.

We're all broken right now, either on one side of the screen or the other. I wish we could drop our phones, look each other in the eye, and love again as God intended.

> *"Above all, love each other deeply because love covers over a multitude of sins." --1 Peter 4:8 NIV*

Lord, I want to be remembered as a person who loved. Everything else is just details. Help me to clear my schedule for the things that matter–people. Amen.

Breaking Laws

I turned onto the blacktop and carefully checked my speed as I accelerated.

As I did, my mind pulled up a memory from long ago when a deputy had shown mercy to me. Late for church, I had been going too fast on this same road when he pulled me over. I embarrassedly apologized, telling him I was late for church.

I *was* late. I deserved the ticket. I didn't get what I deserved. That's mercy.

Several years later, I was leading worship at that same church when I saw my college-age daughter enter and sink into the back row. She looked distraught. Throughout the sermon, I glanced her way and wondered why she looked so overwhelmed. Unusual for her, she left the church as soon as it was over and didn't even speak to me.

That afternoon, I sat down to call her but decided to check my email first. Waiting in my inbox was a long letter explaining the look I had witnessed on her face.

She, too, had been caught speeding on that same road but was administered the consequences in a costly ticket. She was ashamed, embarrassed, and afraid to come to me. Still on our insurance coverage, she apologized profusely, knowing my insurance would go up. She promised to pay for the ticket.

My heart broke that she had been afraid to come to me. Her remorse was proof enough that she had learned from her mistake. I called her immediately that afternoon and worked through the details, reconciling our situation.

Several years later, we experienced a similar situation with our younger daughter. Also, on our insurance, she had been negligent in a parking lot and hit a parked car. Rather than tell us she had spent much of her money repairing the other vehicle, she essentially hid the situation.

Both girls were ashamed and remorseful, yet were afraid to come to us for help to fix their mistakes. Instead, they chose to hide it as long as they could.

Oh, how I remember the feeling.

It was a cold night. My kids were at their dad's for the next couple of days. I lay in my bed, alone, unable to sleep. The feeling nagged at me. Memories haunted me. My heart filled with regret and self-loathing until I could take it no more. The darkness closed in on me, filling me with a fear that I had ruined any chance of being forgiven.

I had gone too far.

I had been the one person who could out sin God's grace. I was not eligible for any of His promises now. God didn't want to hear from me; I didn't deserve Him and was afraid to approach Him.

I cried out. I screamed. I beat my fists on my bed. I yelled out over and over that I was sorry. I cried until my body ached and reached the point of being unable to produce tears. I hyperventilated.

I had let Satan sabotage my life. I don't know of a more desperate feeling than to acknowledge that.

My kids now live in two houses. My marriage was over. I had made horrendously bad choices. My life was a mess.

But why now? Why did I feel it was time to come home tonight? Why did it feel overwhelmingly critical to go to Him now, confess, and beg to return?

I had no explanation.

I had ignored the great divide in our relationship for a long time. I had been afraid even to pray. I hid in my stained garments behind my shame. As exhaustion settled in, the room grew quiet.

A calmness filled me. Peace overcame. It took a while to understand what had happened that night. It took ten years to grasp what had taken place fully.

The 15th chapter of the Gospel of Luke, the parable of the lost coin, the lost sheep, and the prodigal son, fills my mind now.

The woman diligently sweeps the entire house to find that one coin. It was that valuable.

The Shepherd leaves the other 99 to find that one sheep; it was that precious.

The father kills the fattened calf and celebrates the son that returns.

His Father treasured him.

God pursued me. He came after **me.** He wanted me back, and even at my lowest, He still loved me. Not only that, but He rejoiced when He finally reached me.

In His eyes, I was that precious.

Oh, how I've learned to love myself again from a God who loved me, regardless.

I made it to church this morning without speeding. I've learned a lot in the past 25 years, but I've also known that sometimes I need reminders. As we stood to sing, we sang of God's "reckless love."

There's no shadow You won't light up
Mountain You won't climb up
Coming after me
There's no wall You won't kick down
Lie You won't tear down
Coming after me
Oh, the overwhelming, never-ending, reckless love of God

Oh, it chases me down, fights 'til I'm found, leaves the ninety-nine. I couldn't earn it; I don't
deserve it. Still, You give Yourself away.
Oh, the overwhelming, never-ending, reckless love of God. 2

I didn't get what I deserved. Instead, I received the reckless love of God administered in the form of mercy.

I will spend the rest of my life living forever grateful.

> *"And I pray that you, being rooted and established in love, may have power, together with all the Lord's holy people, to grasp how wide and long and high and deep is the love of Christ," -- Ephesians 3:17-18 NIV*

My Loving Father, there is not a day that goes by that I do not thank you for coming after me, breaking down the walls, and tearing down the lies. I am forever yours. Amen.

What's That Smell?

It's happened to all of us.

You open the door to the refrigerator, and a dreadful scent looms from a dark corner. The hunt is on. Sometimes it's easy. Sometimes, it may take a while, but eventually, you find the fuzzy, green, black, unidentifiable object, possibly in resealable plastic ware or a plastic bag.

Ugh. It has to go. Even with your efforts to reclaim a natural aroma in your fridge, it might take a while.

Years ago, as a high school student, one of my part-time jobs was cleaning our pastor's house. He was a bachelor at the time. God bless the beautiful woman who came along and became his loving wife and my rescuer.

One particular day, I was tasked with cleaning out his fridge. To this day, we still chuckle about the items I discarded. Let's just say not even a junkyard dog was interested.

I stumbled across a new look at an old familiar verse today.

It's encouraging, eye-opening, and sends me to self-examination. It's funny how Scripture does precisely what Scripture says it will do:

> "All Scripture is God-breathed and is useful for teaching, rebuking, correcting and training in righteousness," 2 Timothy 3:16 NIV

This scripture comes from Paul, who learned his biggest lesson the hard way. The MSG version casts a fresh light:

THE COLLECTION

> *"Everywhere we go, people breathe in the exquisite fragrance. Because of Christ, we give off a sweet scent rising to God, which is recognized by those on the way of salvation—an aroma redolent with life. But those on the way to destruction treat us more like the stench from a rotting corpse. This is a terrific responsibility. Is anyone competent to take it on? No—but at least we don't take God's Word, water it down, and then take it to the streets to sell it cheap. We stand in Christ's presence when we speak; God looks us in the face. We get what we say straight from God and say it as honestly as we can."* -- 2 Corinthians 2:14-16 MSG

My life is an aroma when I live in alignment with His calling. (For more instructions on how to do that, see the Bible, page one to the end.)

My aroma is sweet to Him and those headed in the same direction, towards Christ.

But to those blinded to the truth, true Christians stink.

So we shouldn't be surprised when we're not greeted with open arms.

But yet, we are called to love.

On the flip side, if I say I'm a Christian and my motives aren't pure, then I stink, also. But like that unidentifiable object in the fridge, sometimes it can stay hidden for a long time. Unfortunately, it stinks up the entire area, and eventually, you either need to get cleaned up or thrown out.

An old familiar hymn comes to mind.

> *"Are you washed in the blood, in the soul-cleansing blood of the lamb? Are your garments spotless? Are they white as snow? Are you washed in the blood of the lamb?"* --Elisha Hoffman, 1878.

No matter where or what you're doing, your life gives off an aroma.

May it be a pleasing sacrifice to God.

"Follow God's example, therefore, as dearly loved children and walk in the way of love, just as Christ loved us and gave himself up for us as a fragrant offering and sacrifice to God." -- Ephesians 5:1-2 NIV

Dear Lord, May I always walk in the way of love. Thank you for being the prime example of what that looks like. May I leave a sweet impression on those around me. Amen.

Asking For Help

****A few times in life, we will feel as if the wind has been knocked out of our sails. After a respected leader suffered a spiritual unraveling of great magnitude, I wrote this to process my broken heart and the pain it had caused so many.

As the band began to play, familiarity caused my soul to quicken. We began to sing.

"For my waking breath for my daily bread
I depend on You, I depend on You
For the sun to rise for my sleep at night
I depend on You, I depend on You" 3

These lyrics came from our theme song from this past summer. Summer camp.
Trying to sing but not exude the emotion, I felt a tear spill and slide down my cheek.
Two months. Life had changed drastically for one of us in just two short months. Life has changed drastically for many. One of the family, but not as in my biological family but as in my Church family. One of the family, but not this geographical church family, but as in the family of God. For three years, I had spent a fraction of my summer with this leader. Energetic, Spirit-led, intentional, kind, and passionate about family were just a few appropriate adjectives. Everyone acquainted would have their own list.

From point A to point B was unexplainable, unfathomable, and unrealistic even to consider. It had happened, though.

The fall.

The unthinkable fall.

The mind-boggling, horrific crime that left us all thinking regretfully, "What did I miss?"
Indeed, each of us considered that our self-absorption had caused us to miss it, to miss the red flags. To miss someone slipping away to an unrecognizable place is haunting. It's a place so dark we cannot go, nor do we ever wish to.
I am only on the outside of the ripples. My heart breaks and aches for all those between me and the one who created those ripples. I can't stop praying for them. I've finally stopped crying, but I never want to stop praying.
But for the ripple maker, or in this case, the eye of the storm, my heart is torn, severed between anger, disgust, disbelief, and compassion.

The one I once knew who shared God's love so fervently to the point of tears is now gone. An unrecognizable, hollow soul remains. There are no words to describe how sad it feels. Once again, it was just a billowing of sad ripples from start to a never-ending finish.

Why didn't we know?
Why couldn't we see?
Why do we work so hard to hide our struggles?
We could have helped.
We could have prevented it had we known the storm existed.
Why are we so afraid to drop our masks and be transparent?
Why don't we call out the troops and say, "I'm sinking here; I need help."
Or even just whisper to one person, "I'm losing it."
Sometimes, our worst enemy is simply ourselves, adorned in a suit of pride.
We have reputations to keep, agendas to fulfill, and boxes to check. We don't have time for the world to know we're going down, and we don't have time to deal with disappointed people.
After a while, the complacency numbs like a drug.
We no longer answer to a higher calling. We just follow a downward spiral.

The longer and farther it goes, the faster the spiral until you finally hit rock bottom.
The damage is done.
The destruction is irreparable.
Life is over as it once was.
Redemption might be possible, but it will never cease the ripple.
It will never erase the damage.

"I need help" would've changed everything.

It would've changed a family, a church, a community's world.

> *"When pride comes, then comes disgrace, but*
> *with humility comes wisdom."*
> *--Proverbs 11:2 NIV*

Lord, I don't understand many things in life. Help us to be translucent with each other. Help us to reach out when we need help, even if it means admitting we have sinned and have failed areas in our lives. You have shown us many times what you can do with failures. Thank you for putting my broken pieces back together. Amen.

Blessed Are Those

The Beatitudes.
The full meal deal will land you in Matthew 5. There's so much there to chew on. An abridged version appears in Luke 6.
Breaking them down a bit, I once again lingered on the last one.

> *"Blessed are you when others revile you and persecute you and utter all kinds of evil against you falsely on my account. Rejoice and be glad."*
> *--Matthew 5:11 NIV*

When I picture persecution, I picture harsh and even worse. I envision stories of the persecuted church around the world. I imagine horrific murders and stories of people right here in the US who have lost jobs standing up for their faith.
I've never been there; honestly, I don't want to go there. Am I lacking character-building because I've never felt persecuted? Am I not representing the kingdom very well? Have I avoided persecution because some do not even know who I follow?
I looked up the word revile just to be clear; its meaning is to criticize in an abusive or angrily insulting manner.
Well, now we're talking. Maybe I had earned the persecuted badge after all.
A couple of weeks ago, I made a post merely pointing to an expected Christian behavior of kindness in a situation. The comments were agreeable at first. It wasn't long before a couple of acquaintances began to fill the page with political debate. My perception was they were insinuating my kind view was simple-minded and as a "Christian," there was more to be done. I deleted the entire post.
Make a checkmark by Peacemaker. ✔

A few days later, I made another post, and it took five minutes for both parties to dive in again. I felt targeted. Once again, my post had nothing to do with the platform they wished to discuss. In retrospect, I did feel reviled and criticized in an abusive or angrily insulting manner. So yes, ✔ that box. Can I join the persecuted club?
I read the rest of the passage. Rejoice and be glad.
Nope. Remove the ✔. My response had been ruffled feathers and a bit of anger. I deleted them from my friend's list. Now that's mature. In all seriousness, my check marks are merely sarcasm. I do not view the Beatitudes as a bucket list to check off but rather as a life I wish to live.
I have not indeed been persecuted. My heart and prayers go out to those who have reached that season in their walk with Christ. They are the heroes of faith and what helps build the legacy of our Christian faith.
My day may come. For now, I am still at the top of the list, praying to be humble in spirit, mourning the repeating of sins I knew better than, striving to be meek, thirsting and hungering to be all of the above and more than anything, passing out mercy to people who have offended me. God continues to do that every day for me.
I'm glad he can't delete me from His friend's list.
I vow to be more merciful.
That's the least I can do: pass on what's given to me.

"If it is possible, as far as it depends on you, live at peace with everyone."
--Romans 12:18 NIV

Thank you, Lord. Your mercies are new every morning. May I be merciful to those around me. Thank you for our religious freedom; may we never take that for granted.

It's Called Mercy

The call came in…again.
I didn't recognize the number, but it was a hospital, so I answered.
"Uh," …long pause. "Hi, Mom."
It was one of my adopted sons. I'm not differentiating relationships. The word is essential.
"I'm in trouble. I screwed up again. I partied with a friend. I guess I said some things I don't remember. I made threats. I'm losing it. I'm falling apart."
My first emotion should've been compassion. After all, I've been his mom since he was a child. Instead, my mouth in my mind started with the questions.
 "Seriously? Again? You know you can't drink alcohol. You know you have addiction problems. When are you ever going to learn? Why can't you make good choices and avoid things that send you down the wrong path? After all we've done for you, why can't you live like your siblings?"
Those judgmental words didn't come out of my mouth. They didn't have time.
Instead, he informed me they would be sending him to an addiction treatment center. They would call me soon for more information because he had told them I was his biggest supporter. I gulped.
"I don't know why you've always stuck with me," he said. "I don't deserve it."
I thought for a long, hard pause.
"It's called mercy, son. It's called grace."
All of a sudden, the conversation took on a new view.
It was me on the other line, the prayer line.
"God, I've screwed up again.
My mouth, my attitude, my heart.

I don't know why you continue to forgive me. Why do you continue to love me like you do?"
God's words flooded my heart.

"For the mountains may move, and the hills disappear, but even then, my faithful love for you will remain. My covenant of blessing will never be broken," says the Lord, who has mercy on you."
Isaiah 54:10 NLT

"But you, O Lord, are a God of compassion and mercy, slow to get angry and filled with unfailing love and faithfulness." --Psalms 86:15 NLT

I am Christ's because BEFORE I chose him, He chose me. From Ephesians 1:5 NLT

"God decided in advance to adopt us into his own family by bringing us to himself through Jesus Christ. This is what he wanted to do, and it gave him great pleasure."

Unfortunately, I'm going to continue to have my slip-ups. Growing in Christ takes time and commitment. He is faithful to love and forgive. Unfortunately, this son of mine will continue to struggle as he grows. Christ is there to love and forgive. May I follow his example.

"In your relationships with one another, have the same mindset as Christ Jesus: Who, being in very nature God, did not consider equality with God something to be used to his own advantage; rather, he made himself nothing by taking the very nature of a servant, being made in human likeness. And being found in appearance as a man, he humbled himself by becoming obedient to death— even death on a cross! Therefore, God exalted him to the highest place and gave him the name that is above every name, that at the name of Jesus, every knee should bow, in heaven and on earth and under the earth, and every tongue acknowledge that Jesus Christ is Lord, to the glory of God the Father."
--Philippians 2: 5-11 NIV

Lord, forgive me for always jumping into the judgment seat when I know I deserve judgment just as much, if not more.

Thank you for loving us and being the God of first, second, and infinite chances. May we look to you as our example, to love you like you, forgive like you, live like you. Thank you, Jesus, for your sacrifice that we acknowledge and will always be grateful for your gift. Amen.

Chapter 2

Family

As I sit in my back room working on last-minute edits and chapter introductions, my view is distracted by the yellow-potted Kalanchoe in the window. It's been through a wild summer, and its appearance reflects that.

Long gangly stems with sparse foliage suggest that pruning is in order. The branches arch toward the window as if reaching for the sun, yet at the end of each stem, a beautiful yellow flower emerges.
Transplanted in an antique teapot, most gardeners would pitch and start over. The Kalanchoe was a gift at my mother's passing.
There's something symbolic in the ugly plant daring to show its beauty at this point by blooming.
It's the quintessential of life. It resembles mine. So much of my family is not what I had envisioned. There are more struggles than I dare admit and more frailties than imagined.
But yet.

At the end of each branch, a delicate flower is emerging.
Pruning will eventually happen. It's nature's way. I resolve to capture whatever beauty is in the moment. I will embrace each flower for the charm it holds.
Life will always be highs and lows, ebb and flow.
Family is forever, and I will love even when the flower is gone.

Time Travel

I pulled into the driveway and stopped the car. I took a long, hard look at the house.
I closed my eyes.
The three of us kids clambered from the backseat. Still in our Easter attire, we ran through the yard and up to the front door. No need to knock, for no child ever knocks at grandma's. We bound into the house as Mom and Dad followed, carrying a plate of deviled eggs and Mom's homemade chocolate cake.
A small, slim, gray-haired woman stood at the stove.
Grandma.
She paused from making her last-minute preparations for the meal to greet all of us. Grandpa was in the living room visiting with relatives who had already gathered as more arrived.
Easter.

THE COLLECTION

It was warm and sunny, flowers were blooming, relatives were filling the rooms, and the house appeared to grow each time another member arrived.
Everything was right.
Time stood still.

I opened my eyes and saw that the house did not match the memory. My view was filled with broken windows, missing doors, warped siding, and overgrown bushes. My memories had not lived in a long time, and this home had not been loved for even longer. The perfect world where time stood still could only belong to the 8-year-old in the recollection, not the 62-year-old looking at the remains of time passing.

As I entered the back door, I stepped gingerly on the warped, moderately water-damaged floor. The living room, which once held my grandparents, their six offspring and mates, and fourteen grandchildren for holiday celebrations, swallowed me up.
Not only had it happily fit the family and furniture, but I distinctly remember the old upright piano that had sat against the west wall. I had spent hours on that bench, playing and practicing with Grandma, hoping someday I would own one. That bucket list item had turned into an accordion without my consent.
Given generous measurements, the room would still be about half the size of most front rooms today. I shook my head in disbelief at how time had robbed it of its size. Despite all that, the living room had been instrumental in teaching us the love of family and enjoying the presence more than the presents.

As I walked into the dining room/kitchen, I envisioned the improvised table with all of us seated around it. Once in your seat, if against the wall, you were there to stay unless you were tiny enough to crawl under the table for your escape. I recall doing that several times, navigating amongst the knees and shoes to get out. If needed, other smaller tables were set up in the adjoining room and even on the back porch. Laughter, conversation, and respect were learned here. Eat what was served and be grateful, including the mound of mashed turnips I mistakenly took one year thinking they were mashed potatoes.

Grandma and I had spent much time cooking and cleaning in that kitchen. She kept an immaculate house. She was one of the kindest, gentlest spirits I had ever known. I don't remember her ever speaking ill of anyone. She taught me in that kitchen about the strength and discipline it took to control the tongue. These lessons would be something I would spend the rest of my life working on.

I could still picture Grandpa at the table studying his Bible after accepting Jesus at a later age. Grandma's gentle, quiet spirit was instrumental in that change. I don't remember knowing him as well as I wanted to, but I loved him, and it was so important that he liked me. He did. I realized he loved me, too.

One of the steepest stairways I had ever seen was just off the kitchen. I loved playing upstairs with my cousins, but I despised that stairway. The only way I could get down from the upstairs was to sit and go down one step at a time, much to my cousins' entertainment.

I traveled up the stairs, carefully checking each step to ensure the boards still held me. The upstairs only contained two rooms; one wasn't big enough to earn that title. I do recollect a twin-sized bed setting in that room. I would never sleep in that bed, as it was next to the stairway.

The bigger room I remembered was the size of a dormitory. As I peered through the doorway, my eyes could not believe how small it had become. At its very best, it could hold two full-size beds. I shook my head in disbelief, wondering how my grandparents had raised six children in this home.

Memories of staying all night, playing board games with grandma, having your cheek roughed up with grandpa's whiskers when he hugged you, and spending time with grandma in her garden flooded my mind.

Having seen enough of the rundown home that housed so many childhood memories, I decided it was time to go.

I knew there was one last room I had not ventured into.

As I entered the living room, I looked for the tiny bedroom to the left. I remember the Christmas Grandpa had announced that he was sick. I remember the day I missed nursing class to be at the hospital for his surgery and the day he passed in that bedroom. He had cancer. It stole the majority of my mighty grandma's heart.
Despite the courage it took for her to carry on, it wasn't too many years before we lost her as well.
Frozen Hostess snacks in the freezer on the porch, hours of play in the front yard in her beautiful flower aisle, the tractor tire swing that was introduced to every new cousin when they were old enough, gathering eggs, playing in the birdbath water, and picking grapes from the vines will be a part of me for as long as I can remember.

Despite all these, the dilapidated house, the overgrown yard, the missing barn and chicken coop, and the garden that will never be again are all irrelevant compared to what was instilled in me during those formative childhood years.
My grandmother's faith built my mother's, strengthened my father's, and led to my own growth. The legacy passed down is more important than all else.
As I look at my own family and all those who call me Grandma, I am inspired to be as fondly remembered as I remember mine. Soon, the house will be gone, the memories will fade, and the next generation will pass, just like the one before.
But the faith?
That and its fruition is forever.
God willing, it will survive the test of time.

> *"His mercy extends to those who fear him,*
> *from generation to generation."*
> *--Luke 1: 50 NIV*

> *"Start children off on the way they should go, and even*
> *when they are old they will not turn from it."*
> *--Proverbs 22:6 NIV*

*"I have no greater joy than to hear that my
children are walking in the truth.*
--3 John 1:4 NIV

Thank you, Lord, for the legacy my grandparents left behind. It clearly points to you. May I be faithful in continuing to live out what really matters. You, Lord, must be our priority. Amen.

The Wedding

My dad performed his first wedding ceremony last weekend.

Some may think, "So what's the big deal? People do it all the time."

Some may think, "How in the world did an almost 84-year-old man officiate a wedding ceremony?"

Or "Is there anything that man won't do for his family?"

The answer is no; there's nothing he won't do when his family requests it.

With the wound still fresh from losing his wife just one-month prior, this fearless man proceeded to marry my niece and new nephew. The courage it took from him was exceptional already, not to mention talking about marriage when he had just lost his own. I wanted to share an excerpt from the ceremony that he wrote entirely on his own. It's such a good reminder for us all:

"Sam and Chris, I would like to leave you an example that your late grandma and I tried to follow for 64+ years of a beautiful life together.

#1 Don't let the sun set on your anger. There will be times when there will be disagreements. There is nothing too big to be solved right away, but time causes things to grow and get out of hand. Two can't always be right. Don't let pride get in the way.

#2 Always kiss each other good night. This definitely enhances love.

#3 Don't feel like you can do everything alone. The Bible says in Genesis 2:24, "Therefore a man shall leave his father and mother, hold fast to his wife, and they shall become one flesh."

So, Samantha and Chris, this path you are about to start is between you and God. God is always there if you call on him.

As we gather here under the eyes of God, let us also recognize the seriousness of this occasion. Marriage is a sincere commitment and worthy of our reverence."

In our fast-paced world, our elderly can sometimes get dismissed. Insinuations are made that they have timed out. It's difficult to see the respect and reverence I witnessed years ago. Our world changes so fast. It's hard to keep up with the latest and greatest. It becomes harder to do some things that used to be easy.

I applaud my niece for going to her grandpa, who she highly respected and knew contained wisdom.

He had lived 63 1/2 years with the same partner and spent the last ten years of those being her caregiver.

My niece knew that she didn't know everything my father did regarding partnerships, reconciliation in relationships, and being prepared for the long run. He did not disappoint. We can learn so much from our older generation, a generation I am quickly becoming.

So much of life is not learned in a book but in the day-to-day, the mistakes, the consequences, and the reconciliation of relationships.

My prayers and best wishes to my niece and her new husband. May you be blessed with the joy and endurance to make a marriage thrive.

Thanks for honoring your grandpa.

> *"Is not wisdom found among the aged? Does not long life bring understanding?" --Job 12: 12 NIV*

Thank you, Lord, for the longevity of my Father's life and for enjoying moments of celebration. You are so good. Amen.

A Grandmother's Prayer

Sleep, sweet baby.
These are the moments we live for.
These are the moments we wish we could remember forever.
These are the moments you will never remember. But somehow, they will shape the foundation of your soul.

Collapsed in exhaustion, your angelic little body lays softly against my lap and shoulder. Your sweet baby breath warms my cheek, leaving the aroma of pineapple worn from your last meal.
Long baby lashes are accentuated against your smooth, porcelain skin. The deeper the sleep claims your tired body, the heavier you melt into my arms.
Soon, the pacifier is unnecessary and left to dangle from the edge of your soft, curved lips. Slowly, you surrender to the peacefulness of your dreams.
Sleep, sweet baby.
Sleep in peace. Pursue your dreams.
Tomorrow, you will grow up.
And no one knows what tomorrow brings.
As much as we'd like the promise of peace, love, and the pursuant of all happiness, it is not
guaranteed.
Nothing is guaranteed, nor are we entitled to it.
Life is a gift.
A gift containing amenities to be grateful for and miracles to marvel about.
Life also contains reality.
The reality is that not all dreams come true.
The reality is that we live in a fallen world full of evil.

The only control we have is how we choose to act and react to our fellow man.

Sleep, sweet baby.
May you always have arms to hold you.
May you always find peace in your days.
May you always find rest in your nights.
May you pursue your dreams with unending passion.
May you learn to love others despite the times they will let you down.
May you learn to love yourself despite the times you will let others down.
May your actions and reactions contrast the norm and always be full of love, seasoned with grace.

Above all, may you revere your Creator as God most high but know Him as your truest best friend.
Sleep, sweet baby.
You have a world in front of you.
May you learn to be a part of what changes the world for good simply by changing your own corner.
But for now, sleep, sweet baby.

> *"See that you do not despise one of these little ones. For I tell you that their angels in heaven always see the face of my Father in heaven."*
> *--Matthew 18: 10 NIV*

Lord, I am so grateful for each of my grandchildren. What a blessing they are. Please give us the wisdom to raise them according to your words. Amen.

Dearest Daughter

Dearest daughter,

I may not have prayed for you to be my child, but I have thanked God for you every day since you became mine.

I may not have squealed when I saw the line on the pregnancy test, but I treasure the day when our signatures were on the line at the bottom of the paper.

I may not have teared up the first time I heard you say mama, but I went into my room and softly cried when you felt safe enough to call me Mom.

I may not have watched you take your first steps, but I have watched you take many steps.
I watched you walk into many of your first days of school, walk across the stage at high school and college, and walk down the aisle. My eyes spilled the same bittersweet tears they had with all my children.

You are right when you say there are differences between you and my biological children. There were differences in circumstance that I had no control over, but I love you just the same.
Some things are the same, as well.

I have struggled with you, and I have celebrated with you.
I love you.
I disciplined you, and I argued with you.
I love you.
I have apologized to you, and I have taught you.
I love you.

I have swelled with pride over victories and shed tears over disappointments.
I love you.
Sweet Child of mine,
I may not have carried you in my womb, but I have carried you through some of the most challenging times of your life.
You will always be mine, no matter how you came to be that way.
I love you.
Heavenly Father,
Thank you for choosing me. Thank you for adopting me into your family and for the gift of my adopted daughter. Amen.

> *"For he chose us in him before the creation of the world to be holy and blameless in his sight. In love he predestined us for adoption to sonship through Jesus Christ, in accordance with his pleasure and will—"*
> *--Ephesians 1: 4-5NIV*

The One About My Amazing Dad

We were down to four days and counting, and God willing, Dad would be discharged from the hospital. He had shattered his right hip three weeks earlier.
The extended stay in the hospital brought about every complication possible, but I never witnessed his faith waver throughout that valley. He never gave up. His morale remained steadfast, even when mine didn't.
I don't know why I'm amazed at his resilience.
This man's character is what worked his land into a successful farming operation.
It helped raise three thriving kids and sustain a marriage for 63 1/2 years.

His tenacity allowed my mom to continue living out her life and her last days in the home she had shared with Dad throughout their marriage.

Years ago, Mom said, "Get dressed. We're going to church."
That day formed the rest of their lives, developed his character, and formed my life.
My mom and God finished raising my dad.
They did an excellent job.
I'm so proud to be my Father's daughter.

> *"A wife of noble character who can find? She is worth far more than rubies. Her husband has full confidence in her and lacks nothing of value. She brings him good, not harm, all the days of her life." --Proverbs 31:10-12NIV*

Lord,
I will forever be grateful for my Proverbs 31 mom. She lived her life by choice, not chance. May I be found to be intentional in my choices. Amen.

Sixteen with Dreams

As I watched my 16-year-old granddaughter care for her little sister yesterday, I started a conversation.
"So, how many kids do you want to have when you get older?"
She hesitated, "Well... do you know the limit on how many kids you can adopt?"
I laughed and thought of telling her, "When you've had enough." I chose instead to move forward in the conversation.
"I don't know if there is a limit. What do you have in your heart?"
"Well, after I'm married, of course." (My thoughts interrupted again, "Well, don't tell him the plan.")
"I want to adopt older kids who are about to grow out of the system that no one else has ever wanted."
My heart gulped not only at the sweetness of her heart but at all the difficulty she might be signing up for.
"I want them to have a place they call home and can always go to. A place for Christmas and other holidays. I want to give them somewhere they can always feel safe."
She said she would like to have a couple of her own, but she wanted to adopt "a bunch."
This sweet girl was adopted at four. I remember the Christmas she and her brother gave up presents and asked for donations to the non-profit organization Charity Water. She could not explain the story about children having to walk three miles a day for water without crying in the middle of the telling. She was six.
At a time when there doesn't seem to be much right in the world, I was reminded that good still exists.
Good still exists in all of us. Sometimes, we must pull it out from underneath the other rubble and dust it off.

Occasionally, we need reminders from a 16-year-old who will change the world.
Goodness, I love that girl.

> *"Don't let anyone look down on you because you are young, but set an example for the believers in speech, in conduct, in love, in faith, and in purity."*
> *--1 Timothy 4:12 NIV*

Lord,
What a reminder that we can share light with the world no matter our biological age. Please reside in me and allow me to be a light to the world. Amen.

Dearest Granddaughter,

Sometimes, I don't have the words to say at the moment, and sometimes, I don't have the opportunity to say them later.
Last night, I didn't have the words. This morning, I found them. The chance to share them comes in this letter.

I'm sorry you were upset last night. Even though I'm much older, I remember being your age and having those feelings. Even though I don't know the whole story, I love you muchly, and it hurts when you hurt.

Let me share my perspective from the bleachers.
My first view is of a beautiful young lady practicing with her teammates on the court. You are lovely. Since you don't have much to do with being born beautiful, I'll just thank God for that added blessing.

Secondly, I watched you act as a teammate, encouraging your friends while warming up. Should I count how many high fives and smiles you gave, I wouldn't be able to keep a tally. You have your parents to thank for that. They taught you to be kind and to be an encourager. Your beautiful smile comes from the heart. It's contagious; something else your parents instilled in you.

I witnessed you make basket after basket while warming up. It's obvious you have spent hours practicing and that you have a desire to be good at everything you do. You have yourself to thank for that. You have developed a drive to work for your accomplishments. That's admirable. Later, I watched you emerge from the bench and play from the depths of your heart. That is your character. You have God, your parents, your family, and yourself to be thankful for that.
I'm sorry for what made your view so different from mine.

What I saw from my interpretation was a champion. I saw a young lady entering this world with all of her heart. She will make an impact on everyone she comes in contact with.
I could not be prouder.
I love you.

THE COLLECTION

"Therefore encourage one another and build each other up, just as in fact you are doing." --1 Thessalonians 5:11 NIV

"Do not let any unwholesome talk come out of your mouths, but only what is helpful for building others up according to their needs, that it may benefit those who listen." --Ephesians 4:29 NIV

Lord, May I never miss an opportunity to encourage someone who needs it. Amen

Ketchup

I said Amen, picked up my fork, and began to eat. That's when she started.
"Dear God, (she dragged out the name.)
Thank you for this day.
Thank you for Mama and Dadda, and Gwamma Wonda, and Emmy."
(The list went on as she named every sibling and grandparent she could think of.)
I bowed my head and smiled silently with a full heart. Although she wasn't quite two, she was very distinct in her words and prayer.
I don't know if I've ever heard someone so tiny pray so completely.
She had been taught. She had been shown an example, and it had been modeled to her.
I knew I had a small hand in it, but I beamed thinking of my daughter, son-in-law, and this little angel's four older siblings, who had been such good role models for her.
After a few moments, I could tell she was winding down.
The last line came with a bit of a surprise: "Thank you for God. Amen!"
Thank you for God?
I looked up and saw this sweet creature dipping her fork in her ketchup and eating a bite full.
She had just remembered something I was good at forgetting: to thank God for being God.
I knew all the cute acronyms for prayer that reminded me of each step. Don't get me wrong, I dive in some days with deep adoration and praise.
But some days?
Some days I pull my wish list out faster than Ralphie from the Christmas story begging for his Red Ryder BB gun.
Some days, it's just too easy to forget who I'm talking to.
My two-year-old granddaughter had just shown her Grandma up.

The best part, though, was how lovely that actually was. It was the fulfillment of scripture right in front of me.

In Matthew 21:16 NIV, Jesus says, *"From the mouth of children and babies, I'll furnish a place of praise."*

And again in Matthew 18 NIV: *"Truly I tell you, unless you change and become like little children, you will never enter the kingdom of heaven."*

Reminders are good. This one was gentle and unforgettable. Lord, Before I pull out that petition list, may I always remember to thank you, God, for you. Everything else is just gravy or, in this case, ketchup. Amen.

Father's Day Date

Father's Day is traditionally celebrated with family get-togethers, picnics, a day at the lake, or a BBQ. For me, it's always been spending part of the afternoon riding in the combine or tractor with Dad.

The day of honoring fathers has always landed farmers in the middle of wheat harvest, followed by a mad dash to get the beans planted.

Thus, I grew up with an empty chair at our table and transitioned to enjoying the buddy seat beside Dad. A lot of conversation can occur as that combine or tractor makes its rounds around the field.

I have to admit that our conversations have grown and transitioned over the years.

Finding enough content to fill the time frame was sometimes challenging as a young girl. A few times, our relationship was not the healthiest, thus lending to quiet as we rode.

Among the negatives of adversity, there are always positives waiting to be found.

Looking back on the past ten years and all that it has held, I am so thankful for the relationship I have with my father now.

Today, after work, I headed in that direction to find my seat on the tractor beside him as he planted beans. A short call later found the tractor broken down, and tradition just wouldn't happen. Disappointed, I went home.

Tonight, as I crawled into bed, my phone rang. It was Dad. He just wanted to tell me how much he missed our Father's Day date.

I am one of the luckiest girls around.

> *"Listen to your father, who gave you life, and do not despise your mother when she is old." --Proverbs 23:22 NIV*

Heavenly Father, Thank you for the blessing of a wonderful earthly father. Amen.

1 Corinthians 13

Today was a day of ridiculous drivers.
Twice, someone pulled right out in front of me. Three times, I fumed about someone tailgating. The last straw was when someone crossed the center line and headed toward me.
I slowed the car and left the highway. Upset and shaken, I felt threatened.
Lately, I have found myself in the same place emotionally when I scroll through social media: cut off, threatened, and afraid people aren't paying attention to what's going on around them.
As I started home after work, I realized it had been a while since I had visited the Love Chapter. First Corinthians, Chapter 13, has always been one of my favorite chapters in the Bible. It clearly explains what love is supposed to look like.
I frequently need to flip the pages open to the passage and put my name in place of the word love: Rhonda is patient. Rhonda is kind. Rhonda does not envy or boast. This is a great attitude check. Today, I'd already failed verse four, and I was just getting started.
Finding out my sixteen-year-old granddaughter was sitting at the football field waiting for her brothers to finish practice, I texted her when I stopped to get gas.
"You want to grab Sonic with your old grandma?"
Her response of yes contained eleven S's. Somehow, her enthusiasm was already a breath of fresh air.
My short trip to Sonic ended up lasting over an hour.
There was no way I could interrupt her stories, nor did I desire to.
Recently, my granddaughter had worked as a counselor at Camp Barnabas. If you're unfamiliar with Camp Barnabas, it's a Christian Camp for children with special needs and chronic illnesses. After

some talk about cross-country practice, she told me stories about her week at camp.

One included a small bite to her arm that didn't phase her. She told me about her connection with a sweet, non-verbal seven-year-old. Somehow, she knew beforehand that they would have a bond.

She gave my day an about-face when she showed me a picture of the seven-year-old with a huge smile on her face, embracing my granddaughter.

"She doesn't smile. She found me in the pool, hugged me, and the photographer caught the smile."

I gulped back tears as I stared at the picture. I was glad I had sunglasses on to avoid making a weeping mess of myself in front of this mature sixteen-year-old.

After a few more stories, we ended our chat, and I headed home. Tears streamed from my face as I left town, thanking God for this young woman.

I didn't have to read 1 Corinthians 13 today. I was sure I had already witnessed it in my granddaughter.

> *"If I speak in the tongues of men or of angels but do not have love, I am only a resounding gong or a clanging cymbal. Love is patient, love is kind. It does not envy, it does not boast, it is not proud. It does not dishonor others, it is not self-seeking, it is not easily angered, it keeps no record of wrongs. Love does not delight in evil but rejoices with the truth. It always protects, always trusts, always hopes, always perseveres. Love never fails." --1 Corinthians 13:1, 4-8 NIV*

Lord, May I not just read your Word. Please help me to do as it says. Amen.

Chapter 3

Just Jesus

Jesus is the hardest one to introduce. Not just the chapter about him but presenting him to those around me presents a challenge. Sadly, I'm not sure why.

My first acquaintance with Jesus was in the basement of the local Methodist Church. Our church had combined with the only other church in town for Vacation Bible School. We sat cross-legged on the floor in a circle. Our beautiful teacher, also known as my mom, presented a cake pan with sand, water, and a flannel graph figure of Jesus. She told the story of Jesus walking on the water. I was mesmerized. Maybe it was the props or just Jesus.

At age 12, I met Jesus at the altar and gave my life to him. I was immersed in holy baptism. When I came out of the water, I expected to feel different. I didn't. I wondered if this was all there was to it, just Jesus? When my life fell apart, and I ended up down the wrong path, I sat on my bed sobbing, knowing the only thing that could help me was just Jesus.

The older I get, the more I experience, the more I realize that all I need is just Jesus.

He's the answer to the questions, the light in the darkness, the calm to the storm, the quenching of my thirst, the fulfillment of my hunger, and the peace to my turmoil—just Jesus.

Humility On a Donkey

The morning sun rose from the east as anticipation and expectation filled the air. This was the day! People had been talking about this day for some time. In all actuality, people had been talking about this moment for centuries.
He was coming.
A King.
The King.
The King that would restore Israel to its glory.
The King that would release God's chosen people from their oppression.
At any second, he would ride into Jerusalem.
The masses lined the streets. Many carried palm branches, ready to pay homage as the procession started.
They watched.
They waited.
They envisioned the pomp and grandeur that would announce and precede his entry.
And then. Just cresting at the top of the hill, the sight of his stately animal's ears.
A donkey emerged.
The foal of a donkey, to be exact.
And on that donkey sat Jesus.
The one who had been among them.
The one who had healed their sick made the lame walk and opened up the eyes of the blind.
He was accompanied by waving palm branches and shouting,

> *"Hosanna, Blessed is he who comes in the name of the Lord."*
> *--Psalm 118:26 NIV*

Someone had laid coats across the young foal's back for Jesus to sit on. The crowd spread their cloaks on the ground, making a path. Many followed as the remainder continued shouting, "Hosanna in the highest heaven."

This carpenter's son wasn't the king they had envisioned.

They knew the scriptures:

> *"Rejoice greatly, Daughter Zion! Shout, Daughter Jerusalem! See, your king comes to you, righteous and victorious, lowly and riding on a donkey, on a colt, the foal of a donkey." --Zechariah 9:9 NIV*

But they wanted a king ready to go to war, a war to fix what was broken and set the captive free.

Instead, he came on a donkey, signifying he had come in peace. This wasn't how a king of power and wealth would enter the city.

But Jesus wasn't like that.

He was ordinary, down to earth.

He was humble.

They reflected on his conversation with the rich young ruler. He had asked Jesus what he needed to inherit eternal life. Jesus answered that he must keep the commandments. He assured Jesus that he had and asked what he lacked.

> ***Jesus answered,*** *"If you want to be perfect, go, sell your possessions, and give to the poor, and you will have treasure in heaven. Then come, follow me." --Matthew 19:21 NLT*

Obviously, Jesus didn't hold much value in money.

But what about power and prestige?

Again, another conversation between James and John's mother with Jesus. She had requested that her sons sit at the right and left hand of Jesus in heaven. Jesus rebuked her and said they did not know what they were asking. When the other disciples found out, they were indignant. Jesus addressed all of them.

> *"But among you, it will be different. Whoever wants to be a leader among you must be your servant, and whoever wants to be first among you must become your slave. For even the Son*

THE COLLECTION

of Man came not to be served but to serve others and to give his life as a ransom for many." --Matthew 20:26-28 NLT

Jesus valued servanthood over power.
He wasn't the king they had expected but the king they needed. They wanted what was broken fixed; they just didn't realize what was broken. We live in a world today that doesn't know it's broken.
Look up, everyone. Restoration came a long time ago, in humility, on a donkey. Throw down your cloak and wave your palm leaf. He can still fix, mend, heal, and save all that welcome Him.
Lord, Thank you for modeling humility on a donkey, but even greater, humility on a cross. May I never forget the value of that gift. Amen.

He Is Worthy

"Six days before Passover, we have a houseful of guests. At any other time, you might find me fretting and frustrated. Not today. I'm still so elated that we have Lazarus back with us.

I thought he was gone. In all reality, he was gone. I will always wonder why Jesus took so long to get back here. He was just a stone's throw away, but I guess none of that matters now. My brother is alive, and there he reclines at the table with Jesus, his healer, and mine.

This dinner is in His honor, my Lord. There is much to prepare and to do, and today is one of those days when I want everything toust perfect. **He is worthy**.*" Martha*

As Martha finishes the final preparations, her sister Mary enters and sits at Jesus' feet. It has been a peculiar spring. Lazarus is alive. There is gratefulness in Mary's movements, accompanied by actions that even she cannot explain. Beside her lap, she sets the bottle of pure nard. It's a rather large bottle, a pint, valued at a year's wages. It has been in the family for a long while. The reason for its saving has become clear at that moment. She begins to pour it on Jesus' feet, anointing him. As she does, she is overcome with emotion and begins to dry his feet with her hair. Everything Jesus has shown and taught them, love, compassion, power, and forgiveness, become vivid. Mary recognizes **He is worthy**.

Unfortunately, in this world, we are not all given the same eyes. Across the table, Judas Iscariot's brow furrows as he fumes at the frivolous waste.

> *"Why wasn't this perfume sold and the money given to the poor? It was worth a year's wages." --John 12:5 NIV*

THE COLLECTION

Judas's secret life is on the horizon, waiting to be revealed.
Jesus rebukes Judas in a statement that leaves the room puzzled.

> *"Leave her alone. It was intended that she should save this perfume for the day of my burial. You will always have the poor among you, but you will not always have me." --John 12:7,8, NIV*

Jesus is honored. Jesus is anointed. Jesus is worthy.
Heavenly Father, we sing it and we say it, but the full magnitude of it won't be known until we meet you and join the saints in chorus, praising you. Amen

Good Friday

It's Good Friday.
I cried this morning.
Sitting in my back room, reading over the prophetic passages in the Psalms and Isaiah, a particular passage jumped out at me.

I like it when Jesus makes something you already know, something you need to know.

> *"Surely he took up our pain and bore our suffering, yet we considered him punished by God, stricken by him, and afflicted. But he was pierced for our transgressions; he was crushed for our iniquities; the punishment that brought us peace was on him, and by his wounds, we are healed." -- Isaiah 53:4-5 NIV*

When sin entered that day through the fruit, it was a traumatic game changer. The perfect world known in the Garden of Eden separated us from God. Our world became one of struggles, trials, and disease. Not only that, but we would now fight temptation and have to learn to navigate differently. Our world now contains disease and sickness. Hold that thought.

This picture of my mama is from about 20 years ago. Our lady's group at the church had just spent the last year participating in an activity called *Secret Sisters*. We were to wear a crazy hat.
I remember that year in explicit detail. I had drawn my mom's name. Every holiday, birthday, and anniversary, I selected a gift that matched her life and personality, and she received it, having no idea who had given it to her. I conversed frequently with my sister-in-law about her comments after receiving these gifts. She was elated and wondered who knew her so well. Yet, she never grew suspicious of me.
As we went around the circle of women that night, guessing who our sister was, I grew giddy with excitement. I couldn't wait to surprise my mom. I will never forget her words when it came to her turn.
She admitted she had no clue for the entire year, but it dawned on her as she drove down that night. I still remember her words. "I knew it had to be someone really thoughtful. I realized someone that sweet had to be my own daughter."

Surprise ruined, but best words ever!
I miss that woman so much as I look at her beautiful smile and the vibrancy she radiated in this picture. Navigating through the murky waters of Alzheimer's has taken that vibrancy.
Here's where I broke down, not for what has been taken but for what is given. Jesus took it all upon himself. He not only suffered for our sins but also took upon himself our pain, illnesses, and suffering, and he crushed it. He crushed it!

BY HIS WOUNDS, WE ARE HEALED!
Good Friday allows us to reflect and remember the horrific death he suffered on that cross, but soon after, we will reflect and celebrate the

enormous game-changer it was. Death is defeated. Disease and pain will be gone. Sins are forgiven.
What we have lost will be again! The beautiful smile and vibrancy of her soul will be again.
Such love that Jesus displayed on that cross.
I hope you reflect on that and understand why it is called Good Friday.

"Greater love has no one than this: to lay down one's life for one's friends."

Jesus, out of every blessing you have given, your life has been the greatest. Thank you. Amen.

The Man on the Middle Cross

I hadn't planned on going. I've never gone to one before, but stories always circulated afterward. The descriptions were awful. I wanted no part.

Today, I found myself where I had never expected to go. Life does that, doesn't it? Plans to not make plans can always result in, "I wish I'd made plans."
I sat on the hard ground next to a jagged rock formation. So this was it. Golgotha, aka Calvary, aka The Skull. The hill is named after the very resemblance. Fitting to be named The Skull as so many deaths took place here. I took in a deep breath of thick air. It contained a hint that a storm was headed our way. Intermingled with the smell of the storm on the horizon was a mixture of pungent scents: blood, gall, sweat, and something strange, different. If there was a smell the body emits when it undergoes extreme stress, a breakdown of cells, then that's what the last intrusive odor was.

I looked around. The gathering, larger than I had anticipated, was clearly a mixture of all opinions, races, walks of life, and ages. Taunting, jeering, and vengeful insults were hurled at the man on the middle cross. Their faces were filled with hate, as I had never seen before. Their laughter, plentiful in the middle of it all, was maniacal. It was the epitome of bullying at its greatest, teetering on the edge of psychotic. What could one individual have done to cause such hatred?
Off to the side were a couple of small groups enjoying provisions they had packed for the day. As if starved for entertainment, watching a crucifixion was the best thing available for the day. They seemed indifferent, even apathetic.

A couple of groups of soldiers were present and appeared to be doing their job as usual. It was just another workday, just another Friday before the long-awaited weekend. Then there were the mourners. It was obvious that the three women clinging together had been very close to Him. Their clothes and faces showed the wear of a long journey. They were stained with blood, tears, grime, and sweat. Their eyes told of a deep, searing pain inflicted upon their souls. Their pitiful, mournful cries and groaning's should've been enough to stir even the coldest of hearts. It broke me to hear their pain. Amongst them was a small gathering of men. They carried the same emotion but with an air of protectiveness. It seemed projected toward the women but also helplessly at the man on the middle cross. Their sagging shoulders showed hopelessness at the scene before them.

The man on the middle cross. I finally found the courage to glance up at him. I looked away quickly. I swallowed hard, took another deep breath, and shook my head. I laid my head in my hands and closed my eyes. The image continued to be vivid.
Make it go away. Never had I seen flesh so torn, ragged, bleeding, exposed. His body lay open in ripped shreds of flesh. Bruised. Blood from the cruelly placed crown of locust thorns trickled down the unrecognizably beaten image that once portrayed his face.
Suspended against the wooden frame of a cross, three nails held the weight of a full-grown man. Pain and anguish do not resemble what I heard upon each grunt and groaning. The sounds haunted the air as I heard him gasp, pushing against gravity and allowing another small air gasp.
What could any man have ever done to have deserved this?
Who were these deranged people?
What right did they have?
Why didn't they understand?
Even if they didn't know He was our Savior in the flesh, how could they willingly make choices that inflicted such pain?
A heaviness filled my heart, but even greater a heaviness filled my arms now as I found myself standing.
I vowed never to find myself in this position again.
I would be intentional about my plans.
I would have no part in something this horrific.
I am not like these people!

The words no sooner exited my mouth than I looked down.
The heaviness was from the hammer.
I held the hammer.
I had played my part in this crucifixion. I was no better than any of these.
I had shared in taunting and jeers, even if it was modeled in my silence.
Worse yet, I knew who He was when I had picked up the hammer.
"Oh my Lord, what have I done?"
I fell to my knees and laid it down.

I looked up at the man on the middle cross, my eyes locked with his.
His eyes held forgiveness. They held compassion. They were warm.
They spoke without words of a love that had no definition.
The sky cracked open. The rain began to fall.
It felt sweet as it washed over me.
The grime. The smells. The filth. All washed away.
I had been guilty.
I was set free.
I was loved—I AM loved —in one look from the eyes of the man on the middle cross.

Beyond the Veil

The intricacy is mind-blowing. The details are amazing.
The book of Exodus is open before me.
I've been on this journey before. Several times, to be exact. I've skimmed, I've speed read, and I've dismissed details. I long not to do that this time.
My mind is filled with intrigue as I attempt to tackle this book of the Old Testament. Not just reading but now studying and looking into details. After so many years, I long to understand my application and purpose.
The instructions for the layout of the tabernacle begin. Dimensions, number of poles and rings, acacia wood, gold overlay, and placement of items.
How, I ask? Where did these nomads find so many of these crucial materials? I reflect on the journey's beginning, remembering how fond the Egyptians were of their departing neighbors and how the Israelites had gathered gold, silver, and fine clothing to take with them.
Following the tabernacle instructions, guidelines for the priest's clothing follow, including the fine gems used in the ephod and the chest piece.
The lists and rules go on, giving me brain fog. I attempt to understand a culture I know nothing about.
The tabernacle will now be a residing place for the presence of God. For **THE** God. A place for the only God who *is* the Great I Am. The only God who is Holy, righteous, and pure. A place for Him to live amongst them.
Laws must be followed, or consequences will ensue, and they are serious consequences.
The list is ongoing: the sacrifices, the cleansing, the atonement processes. It's so much to remember.

 These preparations are just for the Tabernacle, the Holy Place, and the Holy of Holies.

But then Jesus.
One profound act.
One sacrifice takes the place of all others.
Jesus' death on the cross changed everything.

How many times have I looked at the cross all too casually or even calloused, worn it around my neck, worn it on my shirt, stuck it on my bumper? It's so much more than that.

The veil was torn:

> *"At that moment the curtain in the sanctuary of the Temple was torn in two, from top to bottom. The earth shook, rocks split apart," --Matthew 27:51 NLT*

Complete access was gained:

> *"So let us come boldly to the throne of our gracious God. There we will receive his mercy, and we will find grace to help us when we need it most." --Hebrews 4:16 NLT*

Now I am the residing place of his Holy Spirit:

> *"Don't you realize that your body is the temple of the Holy Spirit, who lives in you and was given to you by God? You do not belong to yourself," 1 Corinthians 6:19 NLT.*

Yet, as I sit here attempting to converse with my God, my humanness stares me in the face. My privilege doesn't seem possible. After all the Israelites had to do to just be near the Tabernacle, and only a few were allowed to enter, I have full access to Him!
I begin to look at my failures. I scrutinize my frailties. I start thinking about ways to perfect myself, become a better person, and clean up my act.
How can His spirit ever reside within me?
Holy reverence and fear fill me—the beginning of wisdom.
The act is done:

> *"For the sin of this one man, Adam, brought death to many. But even greater is God's wonderful grace and his gift of forgiveness to many through this other man, Jesus Christ." Romans 5:15 NLT*

I am a new creation:

> *"Therefore, if anyone is in Christ, the new creation has come: The old has gone, the new is here!" 2 Corinthians 5:17 NIV*

I am no longer condemned:

> *"So now there is no condemnation for those who belong to Christ Jesus." Romans 8:1 NLT*

I am thankful.
I don't want ever to take this access lightly. It came at the ultimate price.

Jesus,
Thank you doesn't seem enough. It's all I have. All I am is yours. Amen.

Rejecting Rejection

I walked to the first station.
"Stand here," the man barked. I stood with my back up against the measuring pole. Nope. Not enough. "Next!" he called to the one behind me. I was dismissed.
I walked to the next one.
"Step up." As I did, I watched the measuring device move. It surpassed the green acceptable zone and moved into the red. I was asked to step down. I moved on and on.
Each station presented another way to measure, calculate, define, assess—-tell me my worth.
Sing into this mic...
Smile into the camera...
Talk to this audience...
Solve this puzzle...
Decipher this problem...
Run this length...
Lift this weight...
The answer was the same every time.
Nope. Next.
I didn't measure up.
I didn't fit the guidelines.
I didn't fit the criteria.
I wasn't what they were looking for.
I wasn't enough.
Simply. Not. Enough.
Their view had slowly transpired and became mine.
Sitting on the couch in my back room, my study guide is lying on my lap. I have participated in an in-depth study about rejection for the last two months. The study forced me to look at moments of

exclusion in my life, my reactions, the consequences that ensued, and what God's purpose was for me.

The last section asked me to recall specific moments of rejection from childhood through adulthood.

Carefully, I examined each situation. Vulnerably, I allowed God to open my mind and heart to see each situation.

Yes, there have been plenty of rejections in my life. Were they really all that different from anyone else? But it was not the rejection but my overall response that had made the difference.

Instead of seeking truth, I had allowed their view to become mine. I had let rejection define me.

I watched myself again as I stepped up to be measured, "Nope, you are not tall enough," I told myself. As I stepped on the scales, "Nope, this is not the desired weight," I whispered. As I looked in the mirror, my eyes grew critical. "Nope, you're not pretty enough."

Activities requiring intelligence. Nope.

My measuring devices went on; the results were always the same. Not fast enough, not rich enough, not wanted enough. I suddenly realized I had no idea how other people felt about me. I only knew how I felt about myself.

The last question in the study? What had I chosen to do with these situations?

I realized the truth wasn't what I had chosen. Fortunately, the reality was HE had chosen me.

In times when there seemed to be nothing but confusion, HE was there. Days when I was lost, HE came after me. HE beckoned me. HE had drawn me. HE had quieted me. HE had stilled me.

I realized as I stood before him that all measuring devices were gone.

I am covered. I am wanted.
HE restores me.
HE makes me whole.
HE fulfills me.
HE inspires me.

HE ignites me.
HE completes me.
In Jesus Christ, I don't have to meet the expectations of this world or the expectations that I place on myself.
HE loves me.
HE died for me.
HE longs to give me eternal life with him. Nothing else matters other than I let that be what motivates me and guides me.
There is no other measuring instrument that matters.

Today, I have cried my last tears and have closed the last page of the book of rejection.
I was crafted by the mighty and creative hand of the Lord Almighty.

I. Am. Chosen.

> *"God the Father knew you and chose you long ago, and his Spirit has made you holy. As a result, you have obeyed him and have been cleansed by the blood of Jesus Christ. May God give you more and more grace and peace."*
> *--1 Peter 1:2 NLT*

Only You

I have read many times that whatever gets the most of your time and attention, whatever takes precedence in your life, is what you worship. As I make my way to work, Crowder plays softly in the background:

"Take my fret, take my fear
All I have I'm leaving here
Be all my hopes, be all my dreams
Be all my delights; be my everything
And I will worship You, Lord
Only You, Lord
And I will bow down before You
Only You, Lord." [4]

In wanting to be completely honest, I scan my thoughts for the past 24 hours. So many friends are suffering right now. My heart breaks for them. I pray. I wait. And I continue to watch them suffer.
God is sovereign; of this, I am sure. But I still let my mind wander and as it runs loose, I struggle with the what-ifs.
So, if this statement is true, sadly, I must confess that some days, I worship my worries, concerns, and anxiety resulting from the worrying. How small my faith looks under this light?
How minuscule do I think God is if hanging onto these concerns is more important than trusting Him with them?
How tightly I clench onto nothing when I could reach for the one who is everything.
Guilty, I find myself at the feet of Jesus.
This is the altar where the worries go. Not the altar that allows them priority to blur my focus and attention continuously.
Once again, I lay them down.

I'm not only acting in obedience; I am trading them for worship. Only God, this God, my God, could continue to have such patience with me. As so I answer:

And I will worship You, Lord
Only You, Lord
And I will bow down before You
Only You, Lord.

> *"Cast your cares on the Lord and he will sustain you; he will never let the righteous be shaken." --Psalms Psalms 55:22 NIV*

Lord, I know you ask us to not worry. I believe. Please help my unbelief. You deserve first place in my life, not worry. Amen.

It's Saturday

It's Saturday. The day the disciples thought all hope was gone.
As they cowered in their dwellings, everything they had believed had died on that cross. It was dark in so many ways.
Fortunately, we know the rest of the story.
If they had only known to look to the Horizon, they would have known that Sunday was coming. It may seem dark and hopeless for you right now. The future may look uncertain.
Don't give up hope.
The same power that rose Jesus from the dead lives in us:

"And if the Spirit of him who raised Jesus from the dead is living in you, he who raised Christ from the dead will also give life to your mortal bodies because of his Spirit who lives in you." --Romans 8:11 NIV

Sunday is coming.

Jesus,
Thank you for the darkness of Friday that brought on the uncertainty of Saturday and ended in victory on Sunday.
He's coming!

Forgiven Much Loves Much

I had just taken a bite out of my Chicken Thai wrap.
My daughter had so graciously brought me lunch. It was a treat. True to her nature, she is thoughtful and generous. I am blessed.
I was summoned to the waiting room no sooner had I laid my food down to take a drink.
"I'm sorry," the receptionist motioned to the woman in the waiting room. She got sick. We need some help cleaning up the mess. "
I hurried to the back room and collected all the supplies I thought I might need.
Deep inside, I planned a small pity party for myself. I had a beautiful lunch sitting in front of me, and now it was getting cold and probably wouldn't look so great after I finished this task. Ugh, why me, I thought.
I returned to the waiting room with gloves and the supplies needed to clean up the mess and the patient.
I was met by a sobbing woman holding a lapful of emesis and apologizing, "I'm so sorry, I am so sorry. I can't believe I did this; it's my anxiety. I'm so sorry."
"Please don't apologize. We all have mishaps. Let's get you cleaned up so you can finish what you came for."
It took a few moments of cleaning, standing, and being on my knees, but I finally got everything cleaned off, cleaned up, and wiped down. She left with the nurse for her appointment.
I don't know what she had come in for.
That doesn't matter.
I don't know why she vomited unexpectedly. It happened. That didn't matter.
Others shared opinions. That didn't matter.
I don't know what brought her to this point.
The problem is… that does matter.

Because sometimes, we don't care.
We just want the world to know our disgust with the mess left before us and the mess someone has made of their lives.
We hide behind our imperfections as we whisper and point.
And sometimes, we never stop to think about what infractions may have started their downward spiral.
We don't care if the scales were tipped against them from the beginning or if they were abused, rejected, or neglected. We just don't care.

But today was different. The woman looked me in the eyes.
She was scared.
She was ashamed.
She was sorry.

For a brief moment, I saw the person with the set of eyes I had prayed to this morning.
The eyes of the Man who forgave me of the mess I made of my own life. The Man who was not only on his knees on my behalf but also on a cross. He cleaned up the mess in front of me and the mess I made of my life, and He loved me.

Because, at the time, that's what I needed more than anything.

Just someone to love me.

> *"I tell you, her sins—and they are many—have been forgiven, so she has shown me much love. But a person who is forgiven little shows only little love."*
> *--Luke 7:47 NLT*

Lord God, thank you for the reminders to look people in the eyes and see glimpses of what you see. I'm so thankful you took the time to see and forgive me. Help me to return that to those around me. Amen.

It's Easter Morning

It's Easter morning. The house is quiet, and I do my best to keep it that way, as my husband worked the graveyard shift last night. I scurry around the kitchen, attacking the tasks for the family dinner ahead as I watch the clock relentlessly. Halfway ready myself, I still need to run a curling iron through my hair.
My mind is scattered as I consider when I must leave for the additional service this morning before Sunday school and church. I had skipped the sunrise, which would have been my first choice, but I couldn't figure out how to check all the boxes.
Down to two minutes remaining before the set time of my departure for church, I realized what I was doing.
I was Martha. So many details to take care of, and joining that was pride. What would people think if I didn't attend the first gathering this morning? More than anything, what would Jesus think?

I've spent the past month studying Holy Week and the crucifixion. Jesus and I have shared many conversations and many tears.
I know who I am.
I am a redeemed, unworthy sinner loved by my Savior.
I know who He is.
He is the epitome of love, forgiveness, understanding, long-suffering and relentless grace.

I took off my jacket and went to my back room.
My study area faces the yard and field out the window.
Birds are singing. The grass is turning green. First buds are forming on the trees. Flowers are emerging, and the over-achievers are already blooming. I picture the women going to the tomb that morning, still clenched in the deepest of grief.

They have only one thing on their mind—tending to their Lord. Giving him what He deserves: preparation for a proper burial.
Their minds aren't overwrought with ham cooking times, whether the potatoes will burn before I return home, and whether I have enough seating. Their minds are on one thing—our Lord.
As I sit in my back room, I feel my body start to relax, and my mind turns to one thing.
Jesus.

As I sit at his feet, I see the wounds caused by the nails. His wrists carry the same scars.
In the quiet, His presence assures me that this is not just a story—this is more than just a tradition.
This is the miracle of all miracles.
God was willing to send his only son to pay the price for our iniquities, loving us through all the second chances we will ever need and dying to save us.
This was what I needed the most.
All else is just details.

> *"Martha, Martha," the Lord answered, "you are worried and upset about many things, but few things are needed—or indeed only one. Mary has chosen what is better, and it will not be taken away from her."*
> *--Luke 10:41-42 NIV*

Lord, Details can be crucial, but they can also keep me away from the most important thing in my life: you. Help me never forget what should always be at the top of my hierarchy of needs.

Chapter 4

Lessons

I voice dialed Dad as I drove the car toward home. A routine for some time now, I spent most of my commute home from work talking to my father. Tonight, he answered quickly, informed me he was in a meeting and hung up. I didn't want to be alone with my thoughts right then. After a difficult situation at work, I found myself trying to make light of it by being funny. I said things about a person I would have never said to their face. A few minutes later, they were in front of me and appeared to be angry. I apologized profusely, only to find out they knew nothing about it. Apologizing only drew attention to my guilt and worsened the situation. This led them to speculate about what I might have said, and they refused to converse with me.

As I drove home in silence, I had plenty of time to listen to the conviction of the Holy Spirit. Scripture reminders of taming the tongue and not letting unwholesome talk come out of your mouth filled my mind.
"What am I? In Middle School?" The lessons never stop. I am thankful for that. If the lessons stop, that means I have stopped listening, and I have subsequently stopped growing. My growth chart has only one goal. I need to be ready for heaven when my time comes. Until then, may I continue to grow from His lessons.

Auschwitz

Auschwitz.
The Exhibit.
Union Station, Kansas City.
We sat in the truck afterward, deciding where to go next. After all, we had the rest of the day and hadn't been to the city for over a year. I couldn't answer my husband's request to where I wanted to eat. I really didn't want to eat.
Honestly? I would like to sit in the corner and cry awhile, if you don't mind. I'm not naive about concentration camps. I've read several nonfiction books through the years, watched some movies, and even wrote my college English paper about Ravensbruck.
But maybe I was younger then. Maybe I didn't get the weight of it all. Maybe it was history that lacked faces and names and dreams and babies. Or possibly I'm older now. I understood what I didn't understand. Or, I look at where society is right now, and I wonder.

I wonder. And I fear.

I listen to true crime podcasts. I enjoy trying to figure out behaviors and how people go from point A to as far as point Z sometimes in their acts and behaviors. I never can grasp how a person can end up as barbaric, cold, and unable to feel as they do.

But to try and understand how an entire society can turn into cold-blooded, torturing murderers based on a lie that you are supreme to someone else? My brain can't go there.

I sat in silence.

We picked a place for lunch, and the lump in my throat subsided long enough to eat. We discussed everything but the exhibit, but eventually, I circled back for all the feelings I had left behind. We discussed what hit us the hardest.

The children.

The mamas.

The daddys.

The shoes.

The list went on.

People. Real people.

At that point, my husband said something very profound. The narrator mentioned the Germans were embarrassed at being defeated in WWI. They blamed the Jews despite the statistics of Jewish participation and deaths.

The landslide didn't begin during WWII. It began with WWI. It began with pride.

Is that where we are now?

In all truth, doesn't most sin or evil exist because of pride?

I look at the stories of the Old Testament. Pride.

I look at the stories of the New Testament. Pride.

I look at my own downfalls. Pride.

I don't know what it will take to fix all the hate in this world right now. But I do know this. We cannot let this happen again.

Genocide. It's as ugly as it sounds. The intentional action to destroy a people—usually defined as an ethnic, national, racial, or religious group—in whole or in part.

Aren't we better than that?

Aren't we bigger than that?

I don't have a happy ending to the story.
I left there thinking I would spend the day being grateful for all that I have. I left instead, heartbroken, praying that there is a better future ahead than the history that's behind for my grandkids.
It is too late for the six million Jews and countless other lives that were lost. But it's not too late for us.
If the opportunity arises to see the Auschwitz Exhibit, don't miss the chance to have your heart broken!
Your grandkids will thank you.

> *"Blessed is the one who always trembles before God, but whoever hardens their heart falls into trouble."*
> *--Proverbs 28:14 NIV*

God, I will never forget the day I had looked forward to studying history and left with my heart broken and my soul sickened. Please give us the wisdom to never repeat those mistakes again. Amen.

The Simplest Lesson

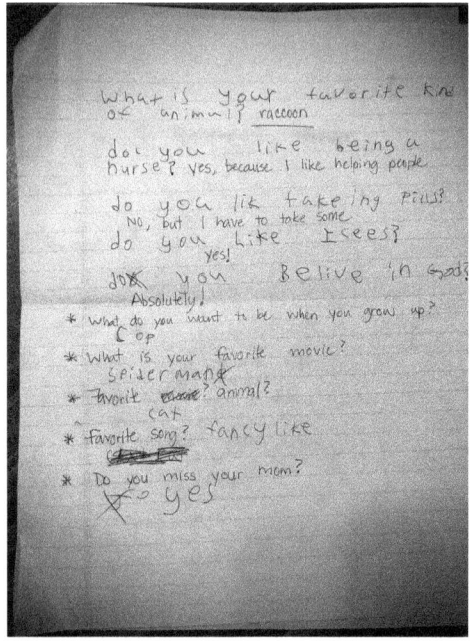

I figured at this age that a grandchild was the only one capable of stealing my heart.
I figured wrong.
I just returned from a week of church camp for 100 fifth and sixth graders. I was the nurse.
A 10-year-old-boy was the culprit. He took a piece of my heart home with him.
He wasn't just any 10-year-old. He was special.
Details are not necessary. Details are irrelevant.
He was special in a delightful way.

As a nurse, he often came to my office for medication. I was curious at first, trying to put the puzzle pieces together. After a while, it became evident that a completed puzzle wasn't necessary.
It didn't matter.
Each visit, he lingered.
One day, he asked what was in the desk drawer. I had no idea, so I opened it and found several small limestone and sandstone rocks.
"Oh, I would love to have those. I love nature."
I gave him a bag of rocks, and he was thrilled.
I was humbled.
I turned around many times throughout the week, and he was there. He never called out or announced his presence. He just showed up.
One day, during rest time, he showed up. He asked if he could talk to me. He said he wanted to tell me about himself.
"Of course," I said, "what's on your mind?"
He came and sat in my office.
"Do you have a notebook and a pen?"
I wondered if he was going to write down his story. Perhaps it was too painful to speak about.
I found the notebook and pen, and he proceeded to write.
He handed me the notebook containing questions for me.
"Here, you answer them and then ask me some."
The game went on for a while. I learned about his love of movies, music, and cats. Especially cats.
One of the most interesting ways I've ever learned to get to know someone was taught to me by a 10-year-old—no electronics involved.
I was humbled.

One evening, he asked me to find the song "Fancy Like" on YouTube. He said it was his favorite. I played it, and he sang along with a big grin.
"Play it again, and I'll show you the moves to it."
The bell rang, interrupting his dance debut. I giggled, thinking about what I must've missed.
On the last night of worship, he asked again if he could sit by me. He always asked permission.
As we stood and worshiped, I could hear his young voice praising God. He looked at me frequently, following my lead.

As we entered into the sermon, we remained standing for the prayer. My friend went to the floor. I just knew he had found a distraction. I tapped him on the back. He didn't budge.
After we finished praying, he got up and sat down. He leaned over and whispered, "That's how I pray."
Gulp.
I was humbled.
My friend didn't make friends easily, but he made one in me.
The chances of seeing him again are a miracle in itself. Promising not to share on social media, I took a selfie with him. It will be my treasure.

Things got a little loud as we sat waiting for camp to be dismissed this morning. I looked over to find him with his fingers in his ears. He was crying.
I asked him if the noise was too much, and he replied, "I just don't want to leave."
I was humbled.
How many times in my life have I experienced that same feeling on the last day of camp?
I realized part of me didn't want to leave either.
Despite the heat, the fatigue, and my sarcastic complaints, where else in the world can you be surrounded by such a force of love?
Where else is the presence of God found so readily and abundantly and never disputed?

God taught me a lot of lessons this week.
Most of them came through the eyes of a little boy.

> *"And he said: "Truly I tell you, unless you change and become like little children, you will never enter the kingdom of heaven. Therefore, whoever takes the lowly position of this child is the greatest in the kingdom of heaven. And whoever welcomes one such child in my name welcomes me."*
> *--Matthew 18:3-5 NIV*

Lord, thank you for the beautiful souls you have placed in my path. Thank you for entrusting their time with me and the gift of memories. You are so good. Amen.

Picking Up the Pieces

As I attempted to remove a broom from the closet, I inadvertently knocked down a puzzle box on the shelf above me...with the broom handle. If it had been a carnival game costing me a dollar to try my luck, I would have never connected.
Nonetheless, the box tumbled to the floor, spilling its 1000 pieces of the puzzle. In retrospect, there may have been 1001.
From far across the room, deep in play and sleep, the 1-year-old, almost 3-year-old child, and "way past his expiration date" dog, respectively, rushed to join me.

To "help," the three-year-old informed me. Yes. That's what we're calling it. The one-year-old managed to dump the box of refilling puzzle pieces at least two more times as the three-year-old played "I Spy" with everything she wanted out of the closet to play with. The dog proceeded to pass gas.
I was able to convince the three-year-old to grab me the hand vacuum, and although I've never liked puzzles, I refrained from sucking them up to discard them.
All I wanted was a broom, to begin with, but I sure made a mess of things. Yep, I've been there. Life always has a way of getting messy in a very short time. Sometimes, it's just a matter of the wrong place at the wrong time. Sometimes, it's the cards or puzzle pieces life throws at us. I've also found myself as the drive-by spectator there to "help." I stand and gawk but don't really do much, and sometimes, maybe even make it worse. We are all too familiar with the parade of cars trailing by, hoping to glimpse the house fire or the wrecked vehicle. Good intentions?
Sometimes, we fall short of the goal to help in our ineptness. The children, in their innocence, meant no harm. They were madly curious. The dog, well, that's another story. In a perfect world, I

would have loved the children to come over, say they were sorry about my mess, and go back to playing, politely staying out of my way. Insert laughter here.

In the adult world, maybe I need to review my ways of "helping." Instead of saying, "I'm sorry, call me if you need anything, or I'll be praying for you," I must be deliberately intentional.
Saying I'm going to pray needs to be accompanied by their name and need in my prayer journal. I need to pray faithfully for the long haul. "Let me know if there's anything I can do" needs to be accompanied by suggestions of assistance and gentle persuasion for them to pick one, even if it's just a pan of brownies. (After all, brownies help with everything.)
I must also be ready to follow up, stay tuned, and stay committed. An encouraging text without a need to reply is something I always relish. I'm sure anything is better than the drive-by spectator mode or, worse yet, the gossip mode. "Just look at the mess she's in."
The puzzle pieces are sealed in a plastic bag and returned to the box, which is now in the closet. The floor is swept. The kids are back deep in play, and the dog continues to pass gas.
It was just another lesson to learn: how to pick up the pieces of life and how we can help others when they drop theirs.
By the way, I found one more puzzle piece an hour later. That puzzle had 1002 pieces.

> *"Share each other's burdens, and in this way obey the law of Christ."*
> *--Galatians 6:2 NLT*

Heavenly Father, Please give me your eyes to see others in need and your heart to follow through. Amen.

Lose the Baggage

The bruises lasted a couple of weeks. The lesson I learned? I hope they last for a lifetime.
I had accepted the challenge of training for a long-distance bike ride. Within the second month of training for Biking Across Kansas, I experienced my second fall.
I don't usually make it a habit to fall when riding a bicycle. Because I was missing my ACL (anterior cruciate ligament) for 45 years, my orthopedist recommended that I cycle with clips. These clips were on my pedals. Special shoes that clip onto the pedal were then worn. They allow the downward push of the leg to propel the bike and the upward motion.
But they can be tricky to get used to. My first fall happened early on when I was just a novice. I had come to the end of an alley when I spotted a car coming. I quickly tried to unclip, and when it didn't happen, I panicked. Within seconds, I had the choice of pedaling into the oncoming car or stopping and falling over with the bike.
I fell over with the bike.
I'm sure it was quite entertaining. After that, I spent a lot of time practicing and making muscle memory of the unclipping process.
I felt confident. At least, I thought I was that day as I took off on my 20-mile loop.
My halfway point was in a local town, and I usually turned around in the parking lot of their Catholic Church. It would be unusual not to find cars in the parking lot.
It was early that particular day when I reached my halfway point, and I marveled at the dedication of the people already at the church to pray. I noticed one car specifically as it was the same model as my previous vehicle.
"Kudos," I thought, for being so dedicated. I meant it.

I started back home, and about 3/4 of the way, I dropped my trusted sweat cloth. It was the perfect size and fabric for keeping sweat out of my eyes. Reluctantly, I decided I had better turn around and go back and get it.

I always unclipped on the left side and leaned in that direction, keeping the right side clipped. As I turned into the driveway to turn around, I noticed a car was coming. I unclipped but inadvertently leaned to the right instead of the left. My bike fell over with me attached to it. Not only did I fall in the mud, but I also landed on a cement culvert in my path.

The car buzzed by. No brake lights, nothing.

I lay on the ground with my right hip against the cement culvert. It was the car I had seen in the church parking lot. It would've been impossible for them to miss my beautiful dismount or lack thereof.

I immediately grew angry. Why didn't the driver stop and check to see if I was okay? Why didn't they at least slow down or indicate that they had considered it?

Next up, I began to judge.

"So you went to church this morning and checked all the boxes but couldn't check on the lady who crashed her bike?"

I fumed for a few days and then let it go, but I would spot the car frequently as I cycled my usual loop.

It remained on my mind for five months.

I think God grew tired of my grumbling. While on the same bike route this morning, the Holy Spirit placed some convicting thoughts in my path.

"If you want to judge people, start with yourself. How often has someone fallen in front of you or been wallowing in the mud, and you've kept going?"

I knew the reference wasn't actually falling or wallowing in the mud but struggling, struggling with relationships, finances, or health.

I took a deep sigh.

I resented the lady who drove a car like mine for five months, and I didn't even know her name, let alone her story.

Maybe she didn't see me fall. Perhaps she was disabled and wouldn't have been able to help me anyway had I needed it.
And maybe she did see me and didn't care.
But that wasn't my problem.
Resenting her was.
It amazes me how far I think I've made it in my Christian walk, only to find I still have pettiness.
Before returning home, I prayed for God to forgive me and thanked him for his sacrifice that gave me that privilege.

"Why do you look at the speck of sawdust in your brother's eye and pay no attention to the plank in your own eye?" --Matthew 7:3 NIV

Lord, I promise I'll watch more closely for people in my path who need help. And as I said amen, I remembered the man who had asked me for a pair of shoes from the free store two weeks ago. I guess I'd better buy some shoes today.

Be An Enabler

I came across a post recently from one of my journals.
It read, "I'm struggling with what happened last week with the man in the wheelchair with one leg."
Let's rewind the story. A fellow church member texted me. She lived in a neighboring town and was at a loss for what to do. Her family had just eaten at a fast food restaurant, and while exiting, they had met a man just outside the front door. He was in a wheelchair, was an amputee, and was stranded. The weather was getting colder. He was from Wichita and needed some repairs done to his vehicle before he could get back home. I don't know the story of how he ended up there or why. At this point, it was irrelevant.
The church member contacted me, hoping our free store ministry could help. I called the number and visited with him at length. I knew he had other serious underlying medical problems, as well as some anxiety.
I couldn't get down there during my work week, but the church exists everywhere, so I made some calls.
After a couple of calls, I was forwarded to a local contact and assured he would help. Here's where my struggle began.
From my journal again:

"I was given the number to a minister in the area. After a short conversation, he instructed me to read a book that argued that many forms of charity are toxic. My first thought?
I'm already reading a book, the Bible."

The man assured me he would get in contact with our stranded friend and would help. I contacted the man in the wheelchair the next day and the day after.

No one had reached out to him.

Then, I downloaded the book to my Hoopla library app and began listening to it. The basis is that, as Christians, we perform many charitable acts just to feel better about ourselves. It points out that we are enablers.
Some of it was factual. I get the familiar adage: "Give a man a fish, and he will eat for a day; teach a man to fish, and he will eat for a lifetime. I understand that. People can take advantage of situations. But let's be honest; we all, through human tendencies, take advantage of situations. But this man was disabled, cold, hungry, and stranded in a small Kansas town without a friend to help.
I **wanted** to be an enabler.
I wanted to enable him to get a hot meal.
I wanted to enable him to have a warm place to sleep, just like I have.
I wanted to enable him to find someone who would work on his car for a small fee and enable him to get back to Wichita.
Yep, you caught me. I wanted to be an enabler.

As I read my book, The Bible, not the one referred to me, I found that Jesus was an enabler.
He went to the cross and died, enabling me to have eternal life.
He is loving, compassionate, and forgiving, enabling me to be forgiven for the times I fall short.
He's blessed me with a wonderful family and church family that enables me to thrive in this world.
He left his word for us, enabling us to find peace and comfort when needed.
Outside of immersing oneself in the Word of God, the popular TV series The Chosen accurately personifies Jesus.

The Jesus I have read about, the Jesus I know, would never have turned away a homeless, cold, disabled man because he had asked for help too many times.
I know because He has never turned away this broken soul writing this story.
Every time I've asked for forgiveness, he has forgiven me. Every time I need comfort, he comforts me. Every time I need, he gives freely.

If you don't know him already, spend some time with Jesus, our enabler. He won't leave you stranded.

"Whoever oppresses the poor shows contempt for their Maker, but whoever is kind to the needy honors God." --Proverbs 14: 31 NIV

Lord, I have not always seen the opportunities you placed before me. Please help me look and watch for people in need. Amen.

Replacing Worry With a Chef

I peeked in on the sleeping princess.
Bless her heart.
Grandma has been missing lately, and the princess has been missing Grandma.
The Grandma, who frequently shows up with games, craft projects, and imaginary characters complete with British and German accents, has left the building. Actually, she has yet to arrive.
In her place, a 62-year-old woman, fraught with worry and distractions, has shown up as her companion for the day. The woman isn't cranky; she is just not present.
A landslide of "life" events with a relative has left her fighting hard to keep her head above the rubble. Phone calls, texts, questions, answers, and decisions have replaced silliness and laughter.
Etched lines grow more profound in the once carefree face.
As I stand behind that face, I think of His words.
Jesus addressed the futility of worry several times, my favorite coming from the sixth chapter of Matthew:

> *"Can any one of you by worrying add a single hour to your life?"*
> *--Matthew 6:27 NIV*

It cannot.
But it can rob us of moments.
It can steal time away.
It can make us unhealthy.
It can turn a memory-making afternoon with a four-year-old into missed opportunities.
It can turn the headache into a migraine.
Worry is a liar and a thief.

It cannot change anything except you.

I've been around the sun several times now. I realize that removing one habit must be replaced with another.

Remove the worry.

Replace it with what? The predictable Sunday school answers sound cliché. But those answers are the answer.

#1 Go to the Scriptures for "go-to" scriptures. Soak up the words of seeking, praying, and finding peace.

#2 Spend extra time in prayer, petitioning a loving God for your needs.

#3. Find a true friend to listen to your concerns.

#4 When you are in the moment, be in the moment.

#5 Embrace what's in front of you and show love.

#6 Bring back the German chef who cooks those meals for the four-year-old granddaughter.

Laugh because laughter is good medicine.

> *"This day is holy to our Lord. Do not grieve, for the joy of the Lord is your strength." --Nehemiah 8:10 NIV*

My Lord, Thank you for reminders of all that you are. It is always enough. Amen.

Distractions

The usual afternoon routine has been to rock my little granddaughter to sleep and then lay her down to sleep more comfortably.

Today, as she melted into my arms and drifted off, I hung on a little longer. I admired her chubby little face and dark eyelashes, felt her soft breath against my arm, and cherished the weight of her sleeping body against my lap. Just for the time, I cherished that moment.

Today is the only day she will be two years old and one day. Tomorrow, she will be two years and two days old, and in a flash, she will walk across the stage for kindergarten, 8th grade, high school, and college graduation.

I know. This darling isn't my first rodeo, or child, or even my first grandchild. I've had several grands walk across those stages already. Each milestone for everyone is bittersweet.

Looking back, all of their little lives have snuck by so quickly. I am grateful for every moment, blessed with a quiver full, but I constantly fight distractions that divert our attention from what really matters. It's so easy to take it all for granted.

There have been too many distractions lately! I don't think it's just my world alone, but I have allowed it. There's no one to blame except me. I admittedly have failed to ask God for extra protection against Satan's schemes.

Thankfully, His word never fails to speak to me when I'm quiet long enough to hear. Just like people, though, sometimes I take those words for granted.

A recent sermon reminded me of a familiar passage:

"Rejoice always, pray continually, give thanks in all circumstances; for this is God's will for you in Christ Jesus. Do not quench the Spirit. Do not treat prophecies with contempt but test them all; hold on to what is good, reject every kind of evil." --1 Thessalonians 5:16-22 NIV

What a reminder to be in the moment, cherish it, be thankful for it, and keep praying. Stay connected with Him constantly. This is what God wants for us!

I had to read that again…" for this is God's will for you who belong to Christ Jesus."

I love the last part. "Stay away from every kind of evil."

Everything that robs us of joy and peace and takes our eyes off him is linked to evil.
So I held on today. I breathed in the moment.

I felt the joy of my life through my family, friends, and church, but more than anything, I felt the most happiness through my relationship with God. He loves me enough to gently remind me of what matters.

This.

Love. His love. Family. Babies. Friends.
For this, I am reminded not to take it for granted. I am thankful.

Jesus, Thank you for the relationship we share and for all the blessings you have given me. Please allow me to stop and enjoy each one. Amen.

The Girl On the Top Bunk

The Hello Kitty blanket covered the small, thin mattress underneath as she perched on her bed. The young girl sat cross-legged on the top bunk. She scanned the dorm with a small notebook on her lap and a pen in her hand. Her face wasn't readable.
The older woman sat on the bottom bunk across the aisle from the young girl. She did not sit cross-legged as her knees wouldn't work that way anymore. Instead, she sat on the side with her legs hanging over the edge.

At first glance, the view was most likely the same for both.
The aisle was scattered with open suitcases, backpacks, mismatched socks, wet towels, and assorted clothes.
The noises were audible and delivered the feeling that the dorm was the place to be. Girls chatted, laughed, squealed, and even made unrecognizable noises. The campers' ages ranged from eight to ten, and adult sponsors ranged from high school to–well, let's just say campers would describe them as "like their grandparents."

The sponsors chatted quietly, helped campers with their hair, made their beds, or spent a few precious moments scanning their phones. The girl in the top bunk sat quietly, not realizing yet what she was seeing. The woman on the bottom bunk sat quietly. She saw what few others could: She saw the girl on the lower bunk by herself, glancing at the gathered groups, but since she had come alone, she remained alone. No one else noticed. She saw a group of girls giggling nervously and occasionally pointing at other girls. By making fun, they hoped to hide their insecurities. The only ones who noticed were those being pointed at and the older woman. She saw the girl whispering to her one close friend, hoping no one had found out her parents had recently divorced. She saw the sponsor, who was still determining if she was qualified to help with camp this week. If anyone knew her home life, they would question why she had come. She saw the girl who feared it might be the night she would sleep-walk again and thought to herself; maybe she should stay awake all night. The young sponsor who felt intimidated by those who had led camp a dozen times before. This was her first time. The sponsor who had a hard time letting go and felt the need to control every girl's movement. She tended to turn militant.

Lastly, she recognized the older sponsor who had spent many summers at this camp but knew she would be treated like she was too old to understand—too old to know people, feelings, God, and life. Yet, she was the one who had been the camper on the top bunk 50 years earlier. She had experienced what the girls experienced at this young age. She had experienced what the sponsors had experienced at the different seasons of their lives. Through the years, she had experienced every age, feeling, failure, and emotion. She had learned. She had grown. She had taken notes in her mental notebook on people and behaviors and how fragile the human spirit can be. Because of this, she had spent much time praying for this week of camp. And because of this, she would climb off her bunk, get out of her comfort zone, and she would love. Because the risk would be worth it all. After all, someday, the girl on the top bunk would evolve to become the older woman on the bottom bunk.

Resolve to be tender with the young, compassionate with the aged, sympathetic with the striving, and tolerant of the weak and the wrong. Sometime in life, you will have been all of these.

Thank you, Lord, for summer camps, for the innocence of the young and the wisdom of the aged. It's a beautiful story, you have told in all of us. Amen.

Nowhere Else But the Heart

"As for me, here is my covenant with you: You will become the father of many nations."
Genesis 17:4 CSB
And this was God's plan.
And Abraham did. But the storybook ending was not to be had yet, or even now.
Unfortunately, humanity doesn't always play by the rules or, even worse, care about the rules.
In 2 Kings 17, the author recaps Israel's history and summarizes the events that led to the Israelites' capture and exile to Assyria.
Reading from the CSB, the Holy Spirit highlighted the text for me.
Verse 32: They feared the Lord,
But, they also made from their ranks priests for the high places, who worked for them at the shrines of the high places.
Verse 33: They feared the Lord,
But they *also* worshiped their own gods according to the practice of the nations from which they had been deported.
Then, verse 35 comes a reminder: The Lord made a covenant with Jacobs' descendants and commanded them, "Do not fear other gods; do not bow and worship to them; do not serve them; do not sacrifice to them. Instead, fear the Lord, who brought you up from the land of Egypt with great power and outstretched arm. You are to bow to him, and you are to sacrifice to him. And in verse 38: Do not forget the covenant that I have made with you. Do not fear other gods, but fear the Lord your God, and he will **rescue** you from all your enemies."
Verse 40 wraps it up:
However, these nations would not listen but continued observing their former practices.
They feared the Lord,

But they *also* served their idols.
I look at the mess the world is in right now,
the mess our country is in,
the mess our state is in,
the mess our county is in,
and the mess my household is in.
If I look closer, I can see the mess that resides in the corners of my heart.
And I ask myself today, am I exactly like the Israelites?
I fear the Lord, **but...**
It's time.
It's time to shine a light on the corners of *my* heart and remove the idols, whatever they may be.
It's time to destroy the thoughts and distractions that keep me from a complete relationship with my creator.
It's time to worship the Lord my God only.
And he will rescue me from all my enemies.
Lord, Rebuilding needs to start. Please let it begin in the heart. Amen.

Chapter 5

Friends

I've had ample time throughout my life to experience friendships. The first friend I remember was my sister. Despite the fights over our bedroom, the chores, and occasionally a boy, we are still close many years later. I am blessed to have her. As life went on, friends came and went. Some moved away; others changed jobs, and sometimes schedules changed, making interaction difficult.

Each friendship has brought many great memories, learning experiences, and the realization that sometimes we don't go away; we grow away. I would not trade any of those memories and moments. They add value to who I am.

The one friend who has remained my entire life has never changed, moved away, gotten a different job, or decided I wasn't worth the effort. His love is accepting and unconditional. He listens when he's heard the story many times before, comforts when he knows my pain is self-inflicted, and loves when I'm not very lovable. I am so grateful for that. I'm grateful for all the friends who have shared their lives with me, but most grateful for the friend who gave His life for me.

I pray I can become a Jesus kind of friend.

It Looks Like Jesus

I hit the end button to the call, laid the phone on my lap, and allowed the tears to gently stream down my face.
Two times this week. I can't ever remember having this conversation with anyone in my almost 60 years of life, even as a nurse, and now, two times this week.
Two very different individuals, different ages, different lives, but one true common thread.
Last week, we made a furniture pick-up from a couple who have steadfastly supported our free store ministry. If something was sitting around and not being used, they wanted it to benefit somebody and have a purpose, so they would always give us a call. Two Christmases in a row, they had blessed several households with new refrigerators. I loved this generous, Jesus-living, Jesus-loving couple.
Upon entering the house, my eyes quickly spotted a Christmas card from a local hospice agency. Careful not to jump to any conclusions, I waited for my friend to explain if he felt the need.
He did.

And it was what I had feared. The cancer was back. The prognosis wasn't good.
While my husband loaded furniture with him, he encouraged me to go into the bedroom and visit with his wife. Masked and socially distanced, I stepped in to visit. Recent treatments had claimed her hair, and a recent heart attack had claimed her continuance of treatments. Laying in bed, she apologized for her appearance. As she spoke of her inner peace, the full life she had lived, and her love of Jesus, I assured her I had never seen anyone so beautiful.
I meant it. Her face radiated deep joy.

She showed more concern about whether there were more items in the basement we could use than over her handed diagnosis. We visited while the men loaded up the furniture. I left after giving her a "virtual" hug and the promise to pray. She assured me that everything would be okay.

The second conversation took place later that week on the phone with an individual younger than myself. Once again, the cancer had returned, and every effort had been made to find a cure. Palliative treatment was the only answer.
I spent half of the conversation muted and stunned. Disbelief, "No, they're wrong," "I'll pray for a miracle," and "No, not yet," ran continuously through my thoughts. I listened as she explained the peace and acceptance she had arrived at. The other half of the conversation was spent laughing.
My friend was always that type of person. Joy exudes from her pores. Witty, sassy, and sarcastic, she always put a smile on my face.
She was also the person who stepped up when someone needed something. She did that for me several times, but my most significant memory is when a family needed a home. God had laid her name on my heart.
I asked.
She answered.
That story lacked the happy ending we all desire, but it didn't diminish the light in my friend. I think we both grew from it. I know I did just from watching her.
As our call started to close, she told me what was on her horizon. "Jesus gets the first hug, and my mama gets the second," she announced with sheer contentment. I gulped back tears at that beautiful vision.

I sat quietly for a while.
Two friends, two conversations, the same week, the same Savior.
I've always struggled with the exact definition of "peace that transcends understanding."
I have witnessed it now.
It looks exactly like what I had hoped for.
It looks like Jesus.
It is.

> *"For now we see only a reflection as in a mirror; then we shall see face to face. Now I know in part; then I shall know fully, even as I am fully known." 1*
> *--Corinthians 13:12 NIV*

Jesus, That day is coming for all of us. May you find us faithful and trusting in your love and peace. Amen.

Some Beauty Never Fades

I stepped out the back door to grab a quick picture before work. Just yesterday, I caught a glimpse of my beautiful maple tree. The sun had cast an enchanting glow through the leaves, but without any time left in my schedule, I sadly declined. I promise I will catch my picture tomorrow.

As I stepped onto the porch this morning, the scene before me revealed a walkway blanketed with about three inches of red, orange, and yellow.

I knew what that meant.

I looked up.

The tree at its prime yesterday was now sparsely decorated with a few leaves revealing its skeletal limbs.

I sighed.

I sat down on the top step and studied the picture before me.

What I had envisioned was gone, but surprisingly, what was in front of me was even more stunning.

My dog came around from the corner of the house and tromped up the walkway to perch in front of me.

We relaxed for a moment.

Transition had taken place. The beauty wasn't gone; it was merely relocated. It was breathtaking as I took it in.

Last night, we delivered a load of furniture from the Orange Swan to a single mom with two children. Her little five-year-old girl was nonverbal and autistic. She was absolutely adorable.

We filled the empty living room with furniture and provided a table and chairs for the family to sit at for meals. Some other items were added, and the small mobile home quickly warmed into a home.

While unloading the furniture, I reflected on the family I thought had donated it. That's not unusual for me to do when making a delivery.

While finishing up, my husband mentioned where the furniture had really come from. I was wrong.
It belonged to a friend who had recently passed away. Her sister graciously donated her furnishings to us to repurpose.
We finished our delivery, and I climbed into the dark pickup. The wound was still fresh, and my eyes filled with tears as I realized these were my friend's things.

Such a beautiful woman, a beautiful life, and gone too soon. Her beauty was still alive in more ways than I could count.

There was beauty in the memories she had left with friends and family, memories of a warm, humorous, and loving spirit, and how she touched people's lives. There was beauty in how she courageously fought her physical battle and eventually surrendered, although winning spiritually in a glorious manner. There was beauty in the generosity her life had modeled that now had transformed a family's empty trailer into a warm home. Beauty that her charming smile and contagious laughter now light up heaven. Most of all, beauty in knowing she has now seen the very face of God. There could be nothing more delightful than that.

During the ride home, I texted my friend's sister to let her know the happiness they had given someone else today. Her response was affirmation that she is just as lovely as her sister.

My friend's beauty will live on long after the leaves are gone.

I sat on my back step longer this morning, soaking in the cooler temperatures and view.

My life and relationships have gotten messy over the past few years, but I still have so much to be thankful for. Next to God, people make life bearable and beautiful.

I am so thankful for my friend's life and the lovely footprints she left behind.

Her beauty hasn't disappeared. It's just been relocated.

> *"He will swallow up death forever. The Sovereign Lord will wipe away the tears from all faces; he will remove his people's disgrace from all the earth. The Lord has spoken."*
> *--Isaiah 25: 8 NIV*

Lord, Thank you for the sweet memories of sweet friends and the promise of eternal life in Heaven with you. Amen.

Praying For My Friend

He called.
I was hesitant to answer.
The last few conversations had been difficult to navigate. His voice had been weak, and his thoughts were clouded.
But today?
Today, he sounded good, almost like himself.
He was getting better!
The treatment was working.

I pictured her face, her earnestness. I'm not sure she will ever know the part she played.
I'm not sure I will ever see the part she played.
She's just three, but when you ask her to pray, she prays.

We had been running errands, so I decided to swing by his house.
"Whose house is this, Grandma?"
"This house belongs to a friend of mine. He's very sick right now. I'm worried about him. He's in the hospital."
I don't even know why I had driven by. I guess I thought it might make me feel better.
"We need to pray for him; he needs a lot of prayers," I said.
A couple of hours later, we sat down to eat, and she proclaimed it was her turn to pray. After going through her gratitude list of loved ones, she began to pray for my friend. Her tiny 3-year-old voice sounded so small at that moment yet so pure and confident.
"And please, God, help my grandma's friend feel better and help him get well."
I looked up after the amen with tears in my eyes. She looked at me matter-of-factly, almost questioning my face.

A few hours later, my phone rang. Even though my friend was still very sick, he told me they had reached a diagnosis and they were starting treatment.
I had no idea if this was true. I had no idea what this moment meant.

A week passed. No word.

Then he called.
When I answered, I understood.
His voice was unmistakable.
He had his sense of humor back.
My friend was back.
The mountain had been immense.
She had the faith of a child.
Her mustard seed had moved the mountain.

> "Truly I tell you, if you have faith as small as a mustard seed, you can say to this mountain, 'Move from here to there,' and it will move. Nothing will be impossible for you." --Matthew 17:20 NIV

Oh, Lord, To have the faith of a tiny seed. Thank you for the way little children lead by example. Amen.

Losing My Friend

It's been a weekend to celebrate: my husband's birthday, a granddaughter's, Mother's Day, and another granddaughter's high school graduation.
Rain has filled up the dry cracks in the ground. Our church service this morning was phenomenal, but a dark cloud hung in the background.

The call came on Wednesday.
I was at work—news of the passing of one of the most loyal friends I have ever had.
I was blindsided.
His month-plus illness had seemingly turned the corner, and he was to go to a rehabilitation unit on Thursday. We had a good text conversation Tuesday and agreed that he should be home by June 8th, his birthday. That was the plan.
But we don't get to make the plan.

THE COLLECTION

He went home sooner than we had anticipated. Approximately an hour after we conversed.
I've spent the past five trying to process.
I've spent the past five reliving stories and hearing others tell theirs.
I've spent the past five wishing I would've–I should've–I could've.
As I posted a picture of my late, beautiful mom for Mother's Day today, I wrote, "May we all leave a legacy worth telling."
It hit me.
That was exactly what you did, my friend.

I remember the time I arrived ten minutes late for my job interview. You hired me and never said a word until I went to leave, when you said, "Let's try to be on time next time."
You were kind.
The time, I wasn't sure how this newly divorced woman would pay her bills, and you took a chance and gave her more sales territory.
You were kind.
The time you forgot my birthday and drove into my driveway at 8:30 that night with a gift, a card, and an apology.
You were kind.
Every time we ate out while making sales calls, you learned our waitress's name and most of her immediate family's before the meal was through.
You were kind.
For every client we ever called on, you found a commonality with them. Every. Single. Time.
And you were kind.
The way you cared about all your employees.
The way the light shone in your eyes when you bragged about your boys and their families.
The way you remembered details because you knew it was important.
The way you knew people.
The way you got people.
The way you loved people.
You were kind.
I know you knew I loved you, friend, but I'm not sure I ever told you all the reasons why.

You were intelligent, brilliant, funny, caring, generous, creative, determined, loyal, and forgiving.
But above all, the world was a better place because you were kind.

> *"Be kind and compassionate to one another, forgiving each other, just as in Christ God forgave you." --Ephesians 4:32 NIV*

Thank you for the gift of friendships, Lord. Thank you for blessing my life with the loyalty of my friend, Lance. May I model that kindness to those around me. Amen.

Saying Good-bye

Today is the day.
A sleepless night but a beautiful morning and sunrise by the "80," as they call it: an 80-acre picturesque hunting sanctuary.
On a last-minute whim and comments made about the beautiful sunrises, my husband and I set our alarm clock early.
Following the GPS, we found the "80" but couldn't reach it. It didn't matter; the sun rises wherever you are, and it's lovely there, too.
We eventually made our way to the land called the "80" by following the other cars.
The friends came, the relatives gathered, and we were honored to honor you.
A few stories.
A few memories.
A few tears.
A few laughs.
A song was sung that spoke to each one of our hearts. We were blessed to call you a Friend.

And left to fill some pretty big shoes are two amazing sons who are already headed in the right direction.

Although the scripture says, "You were made from dust, and to dust you will return," there is so much more to a life than this.
It's the people you meet along the way.
It's the impact you make in their lives.
It's the selfless things you did when you thought no one was watching.
It's the love and kindness you lived your life by.

We know where your final ashes lay.
At the "80."
But there's a better place where your soul resides.

And deep within all of us is a little piece of your heart that we have claimed for ourselves.

"For my Father's will is that everyone who looks to the Son and believes in him shall have eternal life, and I will raise them up at the last day."
--John 6: 40NIV

Lord, Thank you for Lance. Thank you for all he taught me, and I pray he learned from me as well. Amen.

His Church

I wrote this particular piece during the pandemic. The state had ordered a mask mandate. Church members fought against each other rather than joining forces. This particular Sunday became a breaking point for me.

The brown theater seats were cold against the back of my legs. It took all my strength to pull the chair down far enough for me to climb up on it. Then, all my body weight had to be used to move the seat into a sitting position.
Thin wooden seats with a veneer coating built over cast iron frames. This was my first memory of church. This was where I sat in our row, the one our family claimed every Sunday.
I'm guessing I was probably four and always donned in a dress because that's what you wore in the '60s. I loved sitting back far enough in the seat to make it fold up like a taco with me in the middle.

The sanctuary was full of people, most unfamiliar to this four-year-old. Grandma was always among those faces, and many older ones who were always kind took the time to speak to me, complimented my sister and me on our matching dresses, or lovingly patted me on the head.
Always there.
Always faithful.
Every Sunday.
This was my church as a four-year-old.

As I grew up and started school, our Sunday schedule remained unchanged. It wasn't anything I questioned because that's what you did on Sunday. My memories are filled with summers of Vacation Bible School with ice cream in a cup you ate with a wooden stick. Along with that was a mixture of different preachers and the privilege to sing or play my accordion in front of the church. My faith began with stories of Jesus on a flannel graph board and my all-time favorite, Mom, teaching about Jesus walking on water. She used a cake pan filled with water and some sand.

The older faces started to have names. I knew where most of them would be sitting: The Bonines, Lambertsons, Reeds, Stringers, Dulaveys, Shrums, Fergusons, and many more. As I grew up, I was in their homes and came to know their extended families. I was beginning to be part of their family.
A revival in 1973 found my sister and me walking down the aisle to *I Surrender All*. We did surrender—as much as any eleven and twelve-year-old could. Those same loving faces, now considered like grandparents, congratulated us on our decision.
The years passed. Several boyfriends visited my church with me. Missionary dating was the term later coined. I wasn't very good at it. I was okay at dating but not very good at being a missionary.
I eventually was married in my church. Some of the faces of the church family had gone on to a bigger and better place by then, and new faces joined all the time.

Many years have passed since the cold wooden theater seats and ice cream-in-a-cup Bible schools. We transitioned to padded pews and onto upholstery seats. Children, a divorce, another marriage, grandchildren, and various ministries in the church followed. My four-year-old face turned to forty, turned to sixty. A year into a pandemic has now claimed 500,000 lives. We are left worshiping in two separate areas of the church. One with masks, one without.

Last Sunday, as we sang in the sanctuary, the song ended. For about three seconds, if not longer, I heard our other half (through open doors in the gym) finish the song, delayed due to the livestream. A sadness overwhelmed me. Someone politely got up and closed the door.
I swallowed hard. For a brief moment, I realized our separation was more than a door between the gym and the sanctuary. It was a chasm that I lacked words to describe.
A separation between family.
Our family.
The family this four-year-old grew up knowing.
My church.

What does this look like to the next generation of four-year-olds, now marveling over the upholstery chair they're sitting on? The stability of the friendly faces without names are not in their regular seat. Some are in a separate part of the building. My spiritual giants will always be remembered as such—and it was an entire village. Nothing takes the place of godly parents or grandparents, but nothing takes the place of spiritual giants in your church. They are the ones a child experiences every Sunday, faithfully patting you on the head, leading the way on a journey they've been on for a long time, steadfast and committed.
As adults, we all have our own opinions. We're either vocal with them or make them known in our silent actions.

Has anyone wondered what this feels like or looks like to a four-year-old? They might not have an opinion, but the foundation of their faith and memories is being built right now—not when this tragedy is over, or the next one emerges, but now.
Will I be remembered as a kind, faithful face? As they look back on His church, will they see us as a family they grew up with?
I swallow hard again as I'm overcome with sadness.

I only know this.
My family needs reconciliation.
My church needs prayer.

> *"Therefore, since we are surrounded by such a great cloud of witnesses, let us throw off everything that hinders and the sin that so easily entangles. And let us run with perseverance the race marked out for us," --Hebrews 12:1 NIV*

Jesus, The majority of that era has since passed. May we learn from past mistakes and seek to be more loving and forgiving with our church family. You died for the church. Surely, we can live for it. Amen.

Raymond

It seems slightly peculiar for a 13-year-old to have a sparrow as their best friend.
I remember the day. I was in junior high. The janitor walked in, cupping something in his hands, and he gently handed it to me. It was a tiny sparrow. It had fallen from its nest, and as nature flies or doesn't in this case, he could not return. Raymond, our janitor, knew that I had a love for animals. I was so excited to get home that afternoon and walk in with a shoebox, the bottom filled with a small bed of grass and a small chirping bird. Mom didn't flinch. She had been accustomed to me "saving the world," one animal at a time. The list included many raccoons, two squirrels, an owl, a skunk, and whatever dog or cat might appear on our doorstep. My little bird soon became known as Raymond.

Living on a farm, we had an ample supply of ground feed, and I soon found it worked well for my hungry little friend. I started out sprinkling the grain dust into his open, waiting mouth. I was now his mama. I'm so glad he ate the grain and didn't insist on regurgitated worms. It wasn't long until he was eating by himself. His shoebox home moved into a used birdcage that was vacant from a previous parakeet. He didn't spend much time there, though; he loved flying about the house and landing on our shoulders. He loved sitting on the sill of an open window and enjoying the fresh air. Sometimes, he would sit on my shoulder and peck gently on my cheek. Sparrow kisses. At night, it became a habit for him to perch at the top of the wardrobe in my room. He would loudly squawk if he had already gone to bed before I did, and if I turned the light on, I was scolded sternly. His cage soon became just a formality.

One of his favorite times of the day was family meals. He loved perching on my mom's shoulder and enjoying some of her sliced bread.

He was content. I was, too.

It wasn't long until Raymond found that our kitchen sink was his best water source. It had a small leak, so there was always a small puddle of water on the side of the faucet.

Dad fixed the leak.

The water source was gone.

I had no clue.

No clue the water was gone.

No clue what would happen next.

In the grand scheme of things, there are much bigger tragedies than a sparrow dying.

To this 13-year-old, it couldn't have gotten any bigger.

Unfortunately, one person's tragedy can be another person's entertainment. His story found humor amongst my peers. In his search to find water, Raymond decided to get it from our toilet. The bad thing, of course, was that there was no ledge for him to perch on. Once in the water, he was unable to get out.

He drowned.

In the toilet.

Of course, I was the one who found him. Word soon spread quickly at school, and the jokes and laughter started. I endured it and tried to smile pleasantly as if it was funny if your bird drowned in your toilet. It was then that I learned that it is possible to feel all alone, even when you're sitting in the middle of a crowd. Alone with memories they were not a part of.

Alone with a friendship I missed dearly.

Alone with laughter that wasn't mine.

In my peers' defense, they were in junior high and later high school. The story crept to the top of conversations for quite some time, and again, the jokes started.

They didn't know.

They didn't understand.

Through the years, I have never forgotten Raymond. I have reflected a lot on those memories.

There are things I have learned.

THE COLLECTION

Never assume you know what someone is going through if you haven't traveled on their journey.
Recognize that the person sitting next to you may feel all alone even though they are surrounded by friends and family.
Laughter is great medicine, but never when it's at someone else's expense.
My broken heart didn't go unnoticed. I knew that.
My value to the God of all creation far surpassed my little bird, yet even he was known by my God.

> *"What is the price of two sparrows—one copper coin? But not a single sparrow can fall to the ground without your Father knowing it. And the very hairs on your head are all numbered. So don't be afraid; you are more valuable to God than a whole flock of sparrows." --Matthew 10:29-31 NLT*

It's impressive this happened almost 50 years ago, but it is still so clear. I'm blessed to have had a janitor who thought of me when he found the sparrow—blessed to have so many great memories of bonding with God's wildlife and parents who allowed my feral ways. Blessed to know the creator of all things.
Blessed to understand how vital compassion is, no matter what, no matter who. Thank you, Jesus.

The Table

It was just a table.
In the online vacation rental marketing pictures, it appeared to be a vinyl-overlaid wooden table top with mock antique school chairs around it. Cute, but hardly an icon. Hardly the center focus of the room.
It didn't matter anyway. We wouldn't use it. We always ate at the table while the kids were growing up. After they all graduated, we slowly evolved to the couple eating in front of the TV. We were still in the habit of talking to our Heavenly Father before we ate, but not much to each other while our favorite binge-watch was on.

We settled into our vacation home, and that first evening, we found ourselves with plates on our laps as we watched our favorite sitcom. Several times, I glanced back at the beautiful table. I have since inspected it and found the actual table top to be authentic wood and very heavy. The chairs were unbelievably sturdy and beautiful—nothing like the pictures.

The next day, my daughter and her husband joined us for the weekend. The table collected sunglasses, camera bags, maps, and change. In the center, atop a stack of placemats, a heavy wooden bowl contained neatly folded cloth napkins. We spent the afternoon on some adventures and returned to home base to prepare our already marinated steaks. As I prepped side dishes, I eyed the table. Grabbing the placemats and napkins, I began to create a beautiful setting.

That evening, we sat down, prayed, talked, laughed, and looked each other in the eye. The food seemed better than usual. I was falling in love. Just not sure if it was the table or the conversation or with the people I already loved. The next morning found a day filled with trout fishing, stand-up paddle boarding, and hiking. After returning home, I started to pull out food prep ingredients. My daughter and son-in-law politely booted us out of the kitchen and began creating one of the tastiest dinners I've had. At least since last night. They, too, had set the table, and we found the same camaraderie as before. Meal finished, we pulled out a 1981 version of Trivial Pursuit and ended the evening with their version of Apples to Apples. It's safe to say I've not laughed that long in ages. My sides still hurt.

I found that I loved that table and, more than that, the people who had gathered there with me. It centered not only on physical closeness but also on eye contact, conversation, transparency, laughter, and connection. It was all about relationship.

We made great memories all weekend with every activity, but time spent at the table was the highlight.
Relationship.
It's all about relationship.
Nothing different than with Jesus and me.
Sure, he wants us to do the right thing.
He wants us to serve.
He wants us to love others.
But he desires a relationship more than anything. He wants us to gather with Him, talk, be transparent, laugh, and grow stronger together.
Everything else hinges on just that.

> *"Now this is eternal life: that they know you, the only true God, and Jesus Christ, whom you have sent." --John 17:3 NIV*

Lord, To know you. That is what I desire. To not only gather at the table with you but to have honest conversation and to listen to you in whatever form you may speak to me. Whether it is from your Word or from an individual you have sent, Lord, help me to know you. Amen.

Grandma's Path

This was Grandma's path.

When I was younger, I thought this little hand-poured sidewalk belonged exclusively to her. It made sense because the adjacent parking spot did.

I remember waiting from the front door for Grandma to pull up to church every Sunday. She would park on the wrong side of the road, which I was oblivious to. She did this so she would have easy access to the sidewalk. Grandma had suffered from severe foot pain all of her life, and I don't remember her not being crippled.

We would run out to greet her and then walk into the church with her. Just like the parking spot, she had a reserved seat in the sanctuary, as well. She sat there every Sunday.

I didn't get to sit with her every week. That was probably determined by my behavior from the Sunday before.

I loved the seat beside her, listening to her sing the old hymns and being introduced to the alto part. I didn't understand why she sang as she did, but it was beautiful.

I loved her thick black Bible and wondered why she didn't get in trouble for writing in it. She loaned us our own "Bible," First Steps for Little Feet. I cherished that book, the Bible stories it contained, and the pictures. One of my siblings wrote in it, though, but I know it wasn't me.

As I grew older Grandma's row at church grew, as Grandpa started coming with her. He accepted Christ as his personal Savior in his later years, and I know it was one of the highlights of her life.

Grandma's path is still there. The adjoining sidewalk is receiving some much-needed repairs, but I hope this one stays the same. Even though it's not quite visible, I will always know it's there.

Her influence on where to walk is ingrained in my soul. I can't say I've always stayed on that path, but I was always glad to find it again when I had wandered from it.

Grandma has been gone over thirty years, but her influence will always exist.

> *"The righteous lead blameless lives; blessed*
> *are their children after them."*
> *--Proverbs 20:7 NIV*

Thank you Lord, for Grandma Ruby and all the lessons she taught me, simply by living the life she did. I pray my influence will be that big on my grandkids. Amen.

Chapter 6

Be Intentional

I realize I use the phrase, "That's one of my favorite scriptures," entirely too much. There is value, though, in finding scriptures that are the favorite ones that speak deeply into your heart.
I bought a Christian T-shirt thirty years ago. It proclaimed the words:

Carpe Diem, Seize the Day. On the back were the words from Ephesians 5:15,16

> *"Be very careful, then, how you live—not as unwise but as wise, making the most of every opportunity, because the days are evil."*
> *--Ephesians 5:15-16 NIV*

I love this scripture! It's one of my favorites.
For over ten years, I have consistently practiced prayer and study for an hour every morning. This practice was birthed from the adversity of a torn retina that had my nerves too frazzled to sleep in the early morning. My nerves are better now, and sleep is much easier, but the habit has been ingrained, and I am thankful.

I once heard that praying at the end of the day instead of the beginning is like rehearsing after a concert. There is much truth to that. Going into the day, prayed up and with intention is the best way to avoid the mistakes and regrets of life.
Here's to living intentionally.

Use Your Words

It was only a few words, but they had the power to change.
They changed him.
They changed me.
The words had come before I even knew what I was saying.
It started when the man entered the clinic, hoping he might be able to see the dentist. Finding out they were closed, he sat in the waiting room, seeking shelter from the drizzling rain and chilly temperatures.
He was homeless.
He was sick, and he was hungry.

The shelter wouldn't be open until evening. It was 10:30. The man could barely walk but thought maybe he should head that way. A kind receptionist brought him to our attention. After evaluating the medical issues and what could be done, we encouraged him to relax in the lobby and stay warm. A sandwich, some snack items, a protein shake, and a can of cold Coke brought tears to his eyes. He avoided eye contact as he told us we didn't need to do that. Setting out to find a plan to get him to the shelter at the right time took most of the afternoon. He eventually ended up in a private waiting room where he closed his eyes and rested. He turned down the cheeseburger offer but smiled genuinely at the suggestion.
As his ride arrived, he looked up with the kindest eyes and thanked us for making a long, cold day bearable.
That's when it happened. My mouth opened, and words came out that I hadn't even planned.
"I know you would do the same for me."
He stopped.
He raised his head, and he looked me in the eyes.
"Yes, I would. I truly would."

"I know. I can tell. I see your heart."
He smiled. With wet, shining eyes, he turned to go.
"It's gonna get better," I said, "just wait and see."
"Thank you," he said. "It just did."

> *"Do not forget to show hospitality to strangers, for by so doing some people have shown hospitality to angels without knowing it."*
> *--Hebrews 13:2 NIV*

God, I will always remember the day, this man, and your lesson. Was that the day I entertained an angel you reference in Hebrews 13:2? Thank you. Amen.

Still Standing

I stopped at the mirror this morning, just like I always do. It was time to prepare for the day. After adding the bare minimum, I surveyed my view.
"Goodness," were my only words.

Somewhere deep inside my heart, I think I'm still 20-something. As I travel a little further, my body is feeling 50ish. And as I make my way to the surface, yep, there it is—the soon-to-be 62-year-old woman.
My face tells the tale that I have lived and loved life. The rearview mirror remembers the years that have brought me here. So many memories: kids, step-kids, adopted kids, hard work, victories, losses, celebrations, projects, adventures, and embracing challenges. I've earned the view in my mirror; God willing, there will be more wrinkles to come. I will embrace them, for they have a story to tell.
I drove by this old girl this morning and reflected fondly on the many times I have stopped in the past years and snapped her picture or

admired her grandeur. Looking closer, I realized she is starting to show her age brought on by the effects of time, hard work, and the elements.

I love this barn. I don't know any of its story. As much as I'd like to see someone come in and refurbish the barn back to life, I suspect the owner is aging gracefully right along with her. She can live out her last days standing as she always has. If the walls could share their story of the years, I'm sure they would contain animals and warm hay, early mornings and late nights, summers filling the loft with bales, and children playing in one of the most magical playgrounds around.
She has served well.
Isn't that what we all want?
Isn't that how we all want to be remembered?

Not for stunning beauty or how long we could maintain it but more importantly for those around us to know what we have stood for.
To know we have served well.
To know we have lived well and loved with everything we had.
That's what true grandeur is really all about.

> *"However, I consider my life worth nothing to me; my only aim is to finish the race and complete the task the Lord Jesus has given me—the task of testifying to the good news of God's grace." --Acts 20:24 NIV*

Lord, The description of the word vanity begins with the words, excessive pride. This is not who I want to be. I have the task of sharing you with the world. Please give me the wisdom, courage, and discernment on the best way to accomplish that. Thank you. Amen.

My Wagon

I have a new wagon. If you're picturing a red wagon, a covered wagon, or a station wagon, you may or may not be correct. I must be honest with you, I've never seen this wagon. I have no idea what it looks like.

It's directly behind me, but I've made a conscientious decision not to turn around and look at it.

At this point, you might be thinking I might have lost it. Well, that's precisely what I'm trying to do. Lose it.

The Holy Spirit has been kind enough to shine a light on some things that routinely take place in my heart.

The first one is I have an incredible knack for memorizing words that have been said to "hurt my feelings. "As an aging adult, I am finding scripture memorization harder than ever, but at the same time, I have an incredible knack for hanging onto words that I once found offensive to me. How ironic and sad is that? But now that it's been brought to my attention, I have to ask, now that I know what I know, what will I do with what I know?

The second thing He's pointed out that has become increasingly worse in the past two years is the grumbling conversations in the corners of my mind. Rarely do these grumblings ever leave my mouth, but they're in direct conflict with my prayer that the words of my mouth and the meditation of my heart be pleasing in His sight. I know He hears whenever I murmur about one of my brothers and sisters in Christ, my brother and sister, family or friends, or someone in the checkout line at Walmart (outfitted in faded pajamas.)

I know it grieves Him.

So I decided instead of carrying those burdens, I'm just going to put them in the wagon.

As soon as the Holy Spirit alerts me that it's happening, and rest assured, He does, I picture myself taking whatever it is and putting it in the wagon. Frequently, I find myself saying, "Just put that in the wagon."

Feeling better that it's behind me now instead of stuck on my shoulders, it's hard to explain how emotionally freeing it is.

"Put it in the wagon" has become synonymous with "lay it down, "let it go," "it's not my burden to carry," "it's not my business," "just forget it," "Jesus, please take this because it's too heavy for me."

By the time I make it to lie down every night, I have managed to fill my wagon. Wanting to sleep in perfect peace and keep my mind steadfast on Him, I have to do one thing before I can sleep.

Empty the wagon.

After thanking God for the provision and blessings of my day, I start to review what's in the wagon. As I do, I take silly grievances, deep hurts, and offenses from the wagon and lay them at His feet. It was never mine to hang onto in the first place. Unfortunately, I may come across some of the same things in my path tomorrow, and once again, they'll get thrown back in the wagon.

I find that each time I lay something at His feet, it gets a little easier not to stumble on the next day.

Recently, while studying the Old Testament, a phrase caught my attention. Throughout my study, I noticed the words, "They set their minds on this" or "They set their hearts in that direction."

THE COLLECTION

God's people knew He would be the one to fix their problems, but ultimately, they had to decide to turn in the right direction, to intentionally long for resolution.

I know that Jesus will be the one to heal my memorized wounds with amnesia and soften the rough edges of my heart, but I genuinely have to long for it first.

> *2 Corinthians 12:9 comes to mind. "But he said to me, "My grace is sufficient for you, for my power is made perfect in weakness." Therefore, I will boast all the more gladly about my weaknesses, so that Christ's power may rest on me."*
> *--2 Corinthians 12:9 NIV*

I don't know if everybody needs a wagon, but I do know everybody needs a Jesus. They need the real, one and only Jesus, and they need his patient grace.

And I know what that looks like.

> *"Brothers and sisters, I do not consider myself yet to have taken hold of it. But one thing I do: Forgetting what is behind and straining toward what is ahead, I press on toward the goal to win the prize for which God has called me heavenward in Christ Jesus."*
> *--Philippians 3:13-14 NIV*

Lord, May I be reminded daily to take my burdens and pass them on. They're not mine to carry. You paid for them, and I gave them to you. Thank you for taking them from me. Amen.

Choices

This is a sad picture.
Not the fact that this pool is 57 years old, according to resources.
The sad part is that another season has finished.
Done.
Wrapped up.
A few short months ago, everyone anticipated the summer ahead—ballgames, swimming, fishing, boating, barbecues, county fairs, fireworks, and family get-togethers.
It all went so fast.
What remains is just a memory.
The empty pool echoes laughter, squeals, and the sound of the empty diving board bouncing.
The vacated ball diamonds are already overrun with grass and weeds.
The smell of fresh popcorn and hot dogs has dissipated.

The new season is already here.
The school doors are open, and the football fields are full of athletes.
Anticipation is in the air.
But in a flash, snow will be piled on the ground, and the excitement will move inside.
Life stops for no one.

It's hard to believe that some 55 years ago, I took my first swimming lessons in this very pool. Twenty years later, I stood on the sideline and watched my children take theirs. And here I am in the season of watching my grandchildren swim.
I fear if I don't take in every moment, it will disappear without my ever knowing.

Maybe it's because I'm getting older, maybe it's other things.
The brevity of life on this earth is becoming all too clear.
I have lost many of my favorite people in the last few years.
We are all given the same choices.
I am resolving to hold on to the moment a little tighter and focus even more on being in the present.
Because just like the summers past, one day, I, too, will be just a memory.

> *"Teach us to number our days, that we may gain a heart of wisdom. Satisfy us in the morning with your unfailing love, that we may sing for joy and be glad all our days." --Psalms 90:12,14 NIV*

God, Time stands still for no one. Give us wisdom and intentionality to live our days according to your plans and help us to be careful not to waste precious time. Amen.

The Day

The drive starts out dark.
Pitch black. It's quiet.
I watch apprehensively for animals getting ready to make a run for it.
As I drive, I begin the conversation, pointing out everything I know about Him, everything I adore.
I drudge through apologies and disappointments.
The sky slowly begins to lighten.
I petition through family and friends.
I envision their faces, their struggles, and my hopes and dreams for them.
The horizon starts to take on color.
I play the song "I Speak Jesus." 5
I picture friends struggling with loss, fighting cancer, healing from injuries, and lives starting over.
My heart breaks for them. I hand them to Him as my heart kneels at his feet.

The sun begins to crest on the horizon.
I listen to a song telling of the goodness of God.
The heavens light up.
I see his beauty reflected in the sky and in my heart.
Let the new day begin.

> *"He wakens me morning by morning, wakens my ear to listen like one being instructed." --Isaiah 50:4 NIV*

Thank you for your attentive ear every morning and for the instructions you give me every day. Amen.

Love Yourself As Your Neighbor

Shortly after releasing my first book in November 2020, I encountered a new challenge.

I did it again!
Facepalm as I closed the door. I returned to the project I had started before the knock on the door.
Reflecting, I began tearfully to trudge down the path I had been on lately. The knock on the door was a friend picking up a couple of my books for Christmas gifts.
My parting words are embarrassing even now, "I hope they will bless and not repulse."
No sooner had the words left my mouth than I regretted them. Just last night, I saw a friend at the dollar store. She had asked me to sign her book at some point in the future. I told her I would be honored if she promised not to throw it at me.
Wow! The self-deprecation brought me to tears.
I had no idea writing this book would do this to me.
You see, I love just about everybody. Some of you are a little bit harder, but eventually, you will win me over, or Jesus will win me over for you.
But myself? That's another story.
Writing the book wasn't that hard. The Holy Spirit led the entire way. But releasing the book from the clutches of my controlling grasp is another story.
It is in loving myself that I find the hardest.
Before you list all the reasons, quote the scriptures, and tell me how Jesus changed all that, I must stop you.

I know that. I soak myself in it every day. I believe in His grace. Without it, we're all going to hell, and there is no handbasket provided.
I know how much He loves me.
He truly loves me.
He went after me. He pursued me. I've never been so loved.

But on the other side of that, I still struggle. It is hard to forgive yourself.
It. Is. Hard.
And once again, I assume the world will give me what I have given myself. The vulnerability is a bit more than I had imagined. If you read the entire book, you will understand. It is painfully raw and honest as I share my story.
But it was necessary.
I was called to.
I shuffled my feet and made excuses, but eventually, I was obedient. In my humanness, I reason that if I season you all with my self-doubt, it will soften the blow.
Bottom line? What does it matter? Once again, I'm more worried about man's approval than God's. That, in a word, is hypocrisy. Pride.
So I repent.
I start over again today.
I have prayed and prayed over this book:
For God to speak to you as He's spoken to me. For you to long for Him like water on a desert floor.
For you to be blessed by how He shows up every day.
He showed up today.
He told me He loves Rhonda Kane. Despite it all, he loves me.
And He just told me—please love yourself.

Thank you, God.

Lastly, I'm sharing this because maybe someone else out there needs to hear His words.
Love yourself. He does.

"Therefore, if anyone is in Christ, the new creation has come: The old has gone, the new is here!" --2 Corinthians 5:17 NIV

Lord, You know how long I have struggled. Please help me love myself as you do and love others the same way. Thank you. Amen.

Missed Opportunities

June, 2023, I rose to one of the toughest challenges of my life, riding 530 miles in eight days across the state of Kansas. The training, the discipline, the endeavor, and the memories will be with me forever. I am grateful my daughter offered me this challenge.

Sometimes, an incident happens in our lives, leaving us lost in reflection. With Biking Across Kansas in my rear-view mirror, I have pondered this incident for about two weeks.
The BAK organization was kind enough to place SAG (support and gear) stops along our biking route across Kansas. Water, snacks, and simple bike adjustments are their purpose. Occasionally, we might find we were blessed with a Porta-potty. When not, we all found ways to be resourceful, men a tad luckier than women in that area.

A lot of our SAG pullovers were in church parking lots. Maybe they were never asked, but there was never a bathroom available that I was aware of. About mid-week, we pulled into the backside area of a church on our route. It was just the backyard with several storage sheds and some trees. There were no picnic tables or playground equipment. A fellow biker instructed me not to put my bike on the driveway as the church was having VBS, and some parents were still dropping off kids. Not seeing any parents as we refilled our water reservoirs, I surmised Bible School had already started.
Caught up preparing to return on the road, I was jolted to the present when a woman stepped around from the front of the church and began yelling angrily.
"This is inappropriate!"
I glanced to see what had put her in mama bear mode. Her tantrum was over the top and proceeded for at least 3-4 minutes.

As I scanned the area, I spotted one of our male bikers out by the hedgerow. His back was to us, and unless you knew what he was doing, you didn't know what he was doing.
She continued to rant. "I have children here." (Which, in all likelihood, were not at the back of the church with noses pressed against the windows looking out.)
Unbeknown to me and out of sight, the oldest rider from our group had stepped behind a truck to relieve himself. At his age, this task was probably one of the most challenging parts of the ride for him. At this particular moment, his backside was exposed.
He had no idea. We all stood frozen, caught in the crossfire of someone innocently attempting to protect the innocent from the unseeingly innocent.
Quietly, one of our fellow riders walked over to the older man and became his human shield, blocking the view until he was back together.

Ten minutes later, I rode alongside the elderly gentleman on his recumbent bike as we flew down a steep hill.
"Woo hoo!" he yelled. "This is so much fun!"
This was the moment I longed to hang onto. The previous moment had left me sad.

I learned a lot that day.

The church never stops influencing.
We are constantly being watched.
It pays to enter a situation slowly:

> *"My dear brothers and sisters, take note of this:*
> *Everyone should be quick to listen, slow to speak and*
> *slow to become angry," James 1:19 NIV*

Watch your knee-jerk.
Find out facts before you blow in righteous indignation.
Bible verses covey truth:

THE COLLECTION

"A gentle answer turns away wrath, but a harsh word stirs up anger." Proverbs 15:1 NIV

Some opportunities may never come again.
If hospitality had been offered, maybe the situation wouldn't have happened in the first place.

She spoke volumes that day.

I'm just afraid of what she said.

Lord, I am not immune to damaging the church's reputation by my impetuous actions. We need to start each day with intentionality but can only succeed when we seek your direction. Amen.

The Club

Fifty years and three days, she joined the club.
Every member's right of passage is different. For some, it comes suddenly. It may be a car wreck. It may come in the form of a heart attack. For others, it may be slow—cancer, dementia, or any flavor of a debilitating disease. The cause of entry is varied, and the processing of the new membership is diversified, but the ultimate outcome is the same. You are now in the club. Family events are now painful. Church events are difficult, financial burdens are heavier, and decision-making is a tightrope walk. A new year of firsts has just begun. Everything that was once made as a joint effort without realization takes greater effort. And the reminders are present with every breath.

There is no explanation needed for those experiencing the club. Before entering, it was an uncovered mystery that stirred very little curiosity from onlookers. But now it is as real as the empty spot at the table, the un-dented pillow on the bed, and the recliner that never reclines. The rest of us look on. We drop off casseroles and pen sentiments into cards. We pass out hugs like brochures from politicians and say the "right" words. But we do not understand because we are not members.

Members have no other choice but to walk this leg of the journey alone. Yes, others are present. Yes, they care. They love. But they can never understand nor feel what it's like to be a member until they are. We stand at the front of the church. We commit; we say the vows, and the gun goes off. The race begins.
The race of alarm clocks, meal preparation, deadlines, due dates, shared moments, and plans. They pass, and before long, the years are a blur. "Remember when" becomes a staple in our vocabulary as lines and creases

slowly edge onto our faces. Our wardrobe expands to accommodate our waistlines. Retirement becomes a reality. More plans are made.
Life flies by.
And the day comes.
Your membership has arrived.

And just like that, the last casserole dish is washed. The last thank you is sealed and placed in the box. The house is quiet.
You are alone in your new club.
And even though membership is at an all-time high, you are alone.
Fifty years and three days, and it's a wrap.

Where did it go? What were we doing when life passed? Did our loved ones know how much they were loved?
Did they know they were a treasure?
Did they realize minuscule complaining was only that? Did they know?
Questions for only members of the club?
Or questions for all of us?
Every day.
Anna joined the club earlier than most members are expected to arrive. You remember the story in the gospel of Luke when she laid eyes on the baby Jesus.

> *"And there was a prophetess, Anna, the daughter of Phanuel, of the tribe of Asher. She was advanced in years, having lived with her husband for seven years from when she was a virgin and then as a widow until she was eighty-four. She did not depart from the temple, worshiping with fasting and prayer night and day. And coming up at that very hour, she began to give thanks to God and to speak of him to all who were waiting for the redemption of Jerusalem." --Luke 2:36-38 ESV*

Anna's story was different. Her days with her partner had never reached the longevity some are blessed with. Anna had every right to be bitter and depressed and to assume the fetal position in the corner, refusing to rejoin society. But something set Anna apart. When the first season was gone, she continued to look expectantly for something specific on the horizon. She may have looked back occasionally but made sure

she continued looking forward. The wait was long, but her Redeemer was revealed one day, and the waiting was over.
And it will be the same for us.

I am reminded today to remember the vow.
I am reminded to recommit to the covenant.
I want to live like I won't regret.
Forgive others as I should.
Love like there's no tomorrow.
But I also want to keep my eyes on the horizon, on a particular spot that will reveal my Redeemer one day.

And on that day, there will be no more clubs.

"He will wipe every tear from their eyes. There will be no more death' or mourning or crying or pain, for the old order of things has passed away." He who was seated on the throne said, "I am making everything new!"
--Revelation 21:4-5 NIV

God, I cannot imagine a world without pain. We want it to be on this earth. That will never be. Please help us to keep our eyes fixed on you to get through every storm of life. Amen.

My Peace

Have you ever read something dozens of times and missed a keyword? Then, one day, you reread it, and that word jumps from the page.

> *My peace I give unto you.*
> *John 14:27 KJV*

I have read it, sung it, and prayed it—except I missed it. I think the peace that I wanted was "my" peace.

I can't fathom how to find the dividing line between my peace and His peace. But I went to work trying.

My peace comes with conditions. It exists when my prayer is answered, the storm is calmed, the cancer is cured, the evening is calm, the family gathering is pleasant, and the workday is fulfilling.

Yes, I used the promise of peace that had come with conditions. But the word "my" throws itself at me.

My peace I give unto you.

He is not talking about "my" peace but His peace: The peace **He** gives to us.

His peace looks different.

His peace comes from His will, His sovereign plan, and my ability to align myself with that and know it is best.

His peace comes when I lay down my life, plans, and purposes and allow Him to lead the way to be Lord.

The desires of my heart need to be aligned with His:

> *"Take delight in the Lord, and he will give*
> *you the desires of your heart."*
> *Psalms 37:4 NIV*

Last night was a perfect instance. It had been a long 12-hour day at work. Afterward, I headed to my parents to help break up my dad's day. The evening declined into a fiasco that left me at the table in tears. The details at this point are not necessary. I excused myself to the bathroom, and in a moment of heartbreak, frustration, and immaturity, I expressed a couple of words not typically found in my vocabulary–words that I'm not incredibly proud of. Later, I apologized profusely to God, thinking of myself as nothing but a disappointment to Him.
My peace was gone.

That night, as I lay in bed, I prayed. In a moment of compassion, He showed me His view.
It had nothing to do with worrying about legalism or not being disciplined enough to hold back my tongue.
His view showed this child mopping up her tears with her broken heart. His view said, "I know how much your heart is hurting, and I'm here with you."
His view said this will pass. It's not permanent.
His view reminded me that I had been faithful and that, occasionally, life can be pretty hard on us.
My view changed also, revealing His arms wrapped around me and loving me like no one on this earth can.
That. Is. peace.
That is His peace. Thank you, Lord.

Regrets and Ribs

I found myself Friday morning in that place we've all been…in regret. I headed to work, which was my usual routine. I drove, and I prayed. I tried to listen.
"Lord, please give me another chance. I know it's a long shot, but somehow, someway, put that woman in my path again, please. This time, I'll be obedient. "

It all started Wednesday when I decided to do a day of work after a day of work. Saturday was Free Store day at the Orange Swan, and God had placed it on my heart to give away hamburger. I set out to find the best price per pound and was hoping to bless 50-60 families with a package. With ten hours of the workday under my belt, I walked into the grocery store. Hindsight tells me now that probably wasn't a great idea. Just ahead of me was a rather large family of assorted ages and sizes. It was apparent Mom had already put in her ten hours as they wrangled over who was riding in which cart with which parent.

Not wishing to take part in their family feud, I passed by and passed judgment.
Caught up in the hunt for the hamburger, I was soon distracted by the great price they had on ribs. Texting my husband, I needed to know how many slabs to buy.
Out of the corner of my eye, I caught the mom heading my way. She was with her allotment of divided children: one sitting under the cart, one in the cart, and two following close behind. As I realigned my focus back on the ribs, I caught bits of their conversation.
One of the kids asked for something. Her reply was tender. She explained that when they finally got an oven that would work, she would be able to do a lot of things she couldn't do now.

I was sure the free store had a stove.
God nudged me.
I nudged back.
"I'm not even sure I heard her correctly," I justified. "I don't know her. How rude would I be to interrupt and ask, hey, do you need a stove?"
God was silent. I didn't feel his urging anymore.
I bought my ribs. I purchased the hamburger and left the store.
And as in any good relay, the baton delivery was smooth as the Holy Spirit started His leg of the journey.
When I arrived home, I told my husband the story. I wasn't finished with my fateful finish before he interrupted and smiled, "So we have a stove to deliver?"
"No. I answered. I screwed up. My moment was there. I clutched.
I knew with certainty the odds of finding that woman was like a needle in a haystack.
Thursday went by. The ribs I had purchased now seemed like a frivolous luxury. Not only did I have a working stove and an oven, but I also had a Pitt Boss grill… and a stove sitting in the free store garage—just sitting.

My disappointment in myself was second to my promise that next time, I would be obedient, courageous, and take chances.
That's how I landed on my Friday morning commute, praying as I drove. I knew I had to go back to the grocery store after work again. "Maybe, God, could you bring her back into the store?" At any rate, I told Him I would do the right thing if He allowed it. I work in a walk-in clinic. Sometimes, we see as many as 100+ people daily from a town of 20,000, not including the outlying area.
I was in the middle of my ordinary day when she showed up, but let me explain: It was actually HE who showed up. For surely, this was a divine moment.

Yes, it was her, the mom from the grocery store. She had come into the clinic. I gulped as tears filled my eyes. I had the opportunity to visit with her. I made sure of it. I told her the whole story. I would've loved to have captured the smile that spread across her face. She rubbed her arm as if warming her shivers. I could relate. We

exchanged numbers, and arrangements were made. I have shared the story a dozen times, but I'm not through yet.
God gets all the glory.
I get the humbling.
And Mom gets a stove.
Is He great, or what?
Want to join me for ribs?

> *"Be very careful, then, how you live—not as unwise but as wise, making the most of every opportunity, because the days are evil." --Ephesians 5:15-16 NIV*

Wow, Jesus. Just wow. This story brings me chills and tears every time I recall your provision, goodness, and second chances. You are amazing! Amen.

Chapter 7

Trust

What exactly is trust? I find myself telling people I trust in Jesus; I trust in God.
Yet, at the same time, the first moment the boat starts to rock, I cower in the corner and ask, "Where are you, Jesus?" "Can't you see me?" "Can't you hear me?"
Trust exists in three different forms. The first is a noun. When we trust in someone, we show *dependence and reliance* on another someone or something.
The second form is a verb. We exhibit the *action* of believing in something. The last form is an intransitive verb, to *place confidence* in something.

I speak the truth when I say I trust in Jesus and God, but sometimes, I'm not all in. If I'm not practicing all three forms of the word, then I am lacking, and it is apparent in my doubt, fear, and worry.
I will spend my lifetime attempting to accomplish complete trust. I'm so thankful that the one I trust is patient with me.

My Requests.
His Answers.

I grabbed my coffee and prayer journal and headed outside. I sat on the back steps and wrapped my light jacket around me.

Amazing weather for an early August morning. I will take it and say thank you.
The sun was still below the horizon, but a light pink glow had already been cast across my backyard.
I began scanning my prayer journal before starting to pray. My habit has been to update my prayer list every three months. The notes, intercessions, and scribblings overtake the page, making it hard to see the request that started it all.

As I scanned the petitions, I thought, "How long have some of these prayers been on this list and my heart?"
Quite honestly, some had been there for years.
I've always disliked the term "unanswered prayers."
What? Are there some prayers that God isn't hearing? No.
In the silence, are there some prayers that he refuses to respond to? No.
Does God have a daily quota for fulfilling requests, and when the quota is met, you better just come back tomorrow and try to be earlier than today? No.

In truth, God hears all prayers and answers all prayers—just not always in the way we want them to be answered. We all know that.
I've been inspired many times by petitions that have gone on for years before God moved. I remember a story of a missionary who

stayed and prayed for 17 years before he saw the first convert in his village. Talk about commitment.

Fervency is important.

A clean heart and hands are important.

Perseverance is important.

Persistence is important. I relate to that widow mentioned in the Bible as sometimes my "begging" resembles pestering yet relentless.

What have I learned in the years of praying constantly and never giving up?

*I have witnessed answered prayers that I had given up on long ago. The neighbor who longed for a child and had to wait eleven years.

The prodigal son who found his way home.

The young woman cured of cancer who now has grandchildren.

I had kept praying anyway, and sometimes I wasn't even sure why. I am always amazed and humbled. Sometimes, it feels like a facepalm moment.

*I've grown in my faith through years of relentless prayer. I know He is capable. I want to be praying within His will. I know His timing isn't mine. I will keep trusting and know that what He has planned is far more than I could ask or imagine.

*I must rely on His promises found in His word as I continue to petition. I know He won't leave or forsake me. I know He doesn't want anyone to perish and has been patient all this time for people to turn to Him. I know the plans He has for me are good.

So what have I gained from *"Rejoicing always, praying continually, and giving thanks in all circumstances...? (1 Thessalonians 5:16-18 NIV)*

More than anything, I have learned that I *long* to be as Noah.

> *"Noah was a righteous man, ...and he walked faithfully with God."*
> *--(Genesis 6:9 NIV)*

Walked faithfully with God. Doesn't that fill in all the other blanks?

All the other questions?

All the reasons to continue?

I long to want the One who can answer the prayer more than I long for the answer.
So, here I sit on this step in my backyard, and He is here.
I will continue to lift up the loved ones I long to return to Him.
I will continue to lift up the barren womb of a beloved friend.
I will continue to lift up a resolution and the healing of our nation.
I will continue to pray that we will humble ourselves, repent, and seek Him while there is still time.
The list is huge. This list is growing. I will continue.

I love our time together in the morning, the way we talk throughout the day, and how patient He is when our conversations are sometimes interrupted by literal and figurative squirrels.
I. Just. Love. Him.
And that in itself is an answered prayer.

> *"Devote yourselves to prayer, being watchful and thankful."*
> *--Colossians 4:2 NIV*

God, thank you for the gift of approaching your throne with confidence knowing you are a friend that sticks closer than a brother. Help me to walk closer with you every day. Amen.

Two Coins

"Sitting across from the temple treasury, he watched how the crowd dropped money into the treasury."
He watched.
Jesus was watching.
After the widow dropped in two tiny coins, he summoned his disciples. He knew there was a teachable moment ahead.
There was a teachable moment ahead for me, as well.
"For they gave out of their surplus, but she, out of her poverty, has put in everything she had, all she had to live on."
As I drove to work, I pondered the passage.
No, I have not given until I have exhausted my resources, but I have tried to be generous. I thought about tithing and other ministries we support. I prayed to find more areas today to be generous.
I had no idea what that meant at the time.

All of us, at any given moment, are the proverbial camel, just one straw away from having our backs broken.
We all carry straw daily. It's what we do.
At the latter part of the day, I received the last straw—you know, the one that broke the camel's back. The details are not as important as the lesson Jesus gave. After all, I had asked for one.
It left me emotionally bankrupt.
All of a sudden, Mark 12 had a different angle. There was so much more to generosity than just money.
Jesus doesn't want just that.
Jesus doesn't want just my time.
Jesus doesn't want just my service.
Jesus doesn't want me to just bake brownies for Vacation Bible school.
Jesus wants all of me.

THE COLLECTION

He wants my heart.
That means going more than the extra mile in every season.
It means the most when it comes to forgiveness and grace. Sometimes, it means handing forgiveness and grace to those who deserve it the least—even the ones who never realized you were carrying a load for them anyway.
Jesus wants you to give even when you think you're empty.
It all comes down to trust.
The widow.
She knew she was emptying her resources. The next meal, the filling of the empty coffer, and the filling of her empty soul would all come from one source.
The man watching.
The one who knew she had emptied it all and gave because of Him.

Frustrated, heartbroken, and emptied, the only thing I had left to give to those who had taken from me was everything he had totally and always given me.
Grace and forgiveness.
And just like the widow, I knew he would fill my cup back to overflowing.

I had asked for a lesson I could learn and live, and as always, He gave.

> *"Give, and it will be given to you. A good measure, pressed down, shaken together and running over, will be poured into your lap. For with the measure you use, it will be measured to you.""*
> *--Luke 6:38 NIV*

God, Thank you for always filling what is empty, replacing what is depleted, and giving mercy and grace, even when I don't deserve it. Amen.

Great Is Thy Faithfulness

I sat down on the bed next to her.
My aunt.
She had suffered a brain bleed a few weeks earlier. Then, a subsequent car wreck.
After acute care, she was now in skilled nursing for rehabilitation.
We traveled to the city to take her elderly dog to visit.
A day of checking boxes, so I thought.
Life is never about checking boxes.
As she laid her head on my shoulder for a picture, she began to sob uncontrollably.
She clung to me. I clung to her.
My mom's sister.
Maybe one of the tiny pieces I had left of my mom.
I broke down.
I held her in my arms, and I cried.
I cried because I missed my mom.
I cried because I didn't want to be an adult anymore.
I cried because in my mind, life shouldn't be this hard.
I cried because attacks on life had been so relentless lately.
I cried because I could.
I left shortly thereafter and went to Walmart to retrieve the things she needed.
I returned.
Amongst a cozy, warm blanket and a few other items was an adult coloring book of scriptures. She didn't show much interest in coloring the book as she did in immersing herself in the words within. She smiled as I read Lamentations 3:23-24:

THE COLLECTION

"Because of the Lord's great love we are not consumed, for his compassions never fail. They are new every morning; great is your faithfulness."

The next few months will be lived through the scriptures, "great is they faithfulness."
I have no answer to where the future will lead, but I am thankful for today's lesson.
He was there yesterday.
He was there today.
He will be there tomorrow.
We will get through this like every other thing that is laid in our path.
Great is thy faithfulness.
All I have needed your hand hath provided.
Yes! Great is your faithfulness, Lord, unto me.-Thomas Obedia Chisholm 1923

Lord, Thank you for never leaving our side when we walk through life's difficult terrain. Help us to recognize your presence, no matter how big or small it is. Amen.

Radical

What is radical faith?
What is a radical ministry?
I fear I've been stationed right next to the door of apathy. You can blame it on the decline of our world, the declining health of family members, the fleeting moments of life, or my mortality. You can blame it on a lack of self-discipline. Those all exist, but please, running underneath it all, blame it on Satan.
At any rate, I've gravitated toward and camped on the banks of complacency.
While scanning social media this morning, I read of an acquaintance who recently lost a close friend. I didn't know her friend. I barely knew the acquaintance, let alone her friend, but the words she used to describe her drew me into her friend's story. Something was wildly magnetic about her and ignited my curiosity. I began to search the net for info on her. Yes, I'm that kind of girl.
I not only found her but I found her blog as well. I settled into a story of her travels to a remote area in the jungle where she would be serving. There were several modes of transportation and difficulties in getting her there. Then, news of an unsettling illness within her own family reached her soon after she had arrived, followed by the evacuation of the village she was staying at. Provisions were slim, and then, subsequently, she could return to that village. The common thread weaved through all of it was her love for Christ and for the people in the jungle to know Him as she did.
Radical faith.
Radical ministry.

I don't know if it felt radical to her or if it was just another day in the life? Was her passion so ingrained within her that it had transformed into her mission? It is heartbreaking for those she left behind but comforting to know her radical faith has crossed over to eternity.

My recent study of Luke has brought up the point that Jesus's mission was radical. He came to save the entire world, not just his little circle. Oddly enough, I have been questioning my little circle lately. For about 3 to 4 months now, in light of recent changes in our world, I have wondered, "What does Jesus want the church to look like?" A building, a group of people gathering weekly, serving others, potlucks, committees, bounce house parties, cliques, clubs, small groups?

My answer to every question–Yes, no, not entirely, not even, but then what? Undoubtedly many found themselves lost when there wasn't a building to go to. I do not debate the value of gathering together with the body of Christ in corporate worship, prayer, and study. It is scripture-mandated that we do not forget to do that. What I do struggle with is whether we are missing something. Am I missing something? Is there something we are not hearing, following, or seeing?

I'm drawn to the word radical like a moth is to the flame. I want to be close enough to see and feel it, but I fear deep down getting close enough to let it entirely engulf me.

I want to change. Satan doesn't want that for any of us.

I want to color outside the lines. I desire to live in a way that mirrors and reflects a Love people can't look away from.

I long to be transformed into a Love that they want to know more about, a Love that they need, a Love that they won't survive if they don't have.

I know about that Love. I can't keep it to myself while I camp in my tent of apathy. It would be wrong. I don't understand what radical would look like for me. With all my being, I do know there is something more.

Time in the wilderness is always beneficial, but taking what you've learned and sharing it with others is what changes the world. Humbly, I pray for direction.

I seek Your face, Lord.

I long to turn away from anything that you see wicked in me.

Please hear my prayer from heaven.

Please forgive my sin and start with the healing of my own heart. Then, Lord, please heal our land.
Lord, do I dare pray? Please show us ***radical***. Show us what you want "church" to look like.

Help us to be the change that we hope to see in this world. I'm pretty sure it looks like this saint who has just crossed over.

> *"And without faith, it is impossible to please God, because anyone who comes to him must believe that he exists and that he rewards those who earnestly seek him." --Hebrews 11:6 NIV*

Deepen my faith, Lord, and allow me to follow through in greater commitment and obedience to you. Help me to be radical. Amen.

How Things Used To Be

Some call it the good old days, or do you remember when?
Some of my favorites: "Remember when our phone was on a party line, and our neighbor would listen in on our conversations? Especially my sister and me when we were on the phone with our boyfriends. Did I say boyfriends? I meant boyfriend.
Remember when we were our Dad's remote control for the TV?
Remember when too much screen time meant binging on Saturday morning cartoons?
I drive back "home" a lot…to Mom and Dad's. I remember the previous landscape and house anchored to my childhood memories. There is no longer a fence on the north/south road where I tied a sock on every quarter-mile post as a runner.
Dad filled in the "hog pond" on the east end of our property years ago. That's where I learned to fish.
Our recreation room, complete with candy-striped shag carpet and a pool table, is now an office. So much has changed as the years move on. But has it?

As I remember the younger me, the middle-aged me, and now the "getting older" me, I recognize the things I've overcome and the things I think I have matured in, but there's still a list of things that haven't changed. For example:
I'm still stubborn. (Thanks, Dad.)
I still get defensive when I feel opposition.
I still hang onto grudges that I know I need to drop.
I still allow myself at weak moments to listen to the wrong voice.
I still fret and worry when I need to pray and trust.
After all the changes in my physical life, it sometimes appears that I'm still the same child I was 50 years ago.

Then I look at my own children. They, too, have many ways they have changed but also many things they are still working through, things they still struggle with.

As their parent, I don't find myself asking them, "Why haven't you fixed yourself yet? Why are you still struggling with this?" I don't find myself loving them any differently.

And that's when I get the true picture of how my heavenly Father feels about me and what His love looks like. It causes me to stop, right in my tracks.

Here I am, still running the marathon called life, finding myself closer to the finish line every day, and knowing that my number one fan is the One who created me, gave up his life on the cross for me, and accepts me as his child, flaws and all. Just because I have accepted him as my savior, I appear blameless to him. I appear completely changed. That change has happened only through the brokenness of his body and the blood of Christ.

> *"Therefore, if anyone is in Christ, the new creation has come: The old has gone, the new is here!"*
> *--2 Corinthians 5:17 NIV*

Lord, I could never thank you enough for the gift you gave all of us by merely accepting you as our Savior and living our lives for you. Amen.

It's All I Have. It's Everything I Have

"Wow, if you don't mind, I'm going to lay this down right here–by your feet.
Thank you, Jesus. That was heavy."

(Deep breath.)

"I do feel better. Thank you. I feel more at ease and peaceful.
Even though I was carrying it on my back, it seemed to be crushing my chest, keeping me from breathing right."
"Ok. So that's it? I laid it down. Now I just wait? And trust? Relax?"
"I like this feeling. The feeling of giving this worry to you and trusting you'll take care of it. That you'll supply my every need."

(Fidget)

I'd better at least check on the situation. See what I can do.
I need to do something. It doesn't feel right if I'm not doing something or if I'm not fretting.

"I'm going to pick this back up for just a second and see if I've forgotten anything that was burdening me. I want to make sure You understand the heaviness I'm feeling, the load I'm carrying, and the people I'm worried about.
If you'd like, I can help carry some of it. It's a lot."

(Pause)

"I'm afraid that if I don't help, I may not like the outcome, and I'll blame myself because I didn't worry enough. Because I didn't help."

(Sigh)

Who am I kidding?

"You are the God of the universe. What can I possibly offer to you?"

"I'm going to lay this back down...again.
I understand that sometimes I don't understand.
But I do understand Who you are.
I know what You want.
I know what I need."

(Unloading my arms)

"Trust. You want me to trust.
Do not be afraid. Have faith.
Put it in your hands.
Lay it at your feet.
Let it go.
Be still.
Don't be anxious.
Pray.
Be thankful.
Give you my requests.
Let your peace guard my heart and mind."

(Sigh)

"You'd do all that for me if I just did one thing.

Trust.
Surrender.
It's yours.
It was never mine anyway."

THE COLLECTION

(Deep breath.)

I. Trust. You.

> *"When I am afraid, I put my trust in you. In God, whose word I praise— in God I trust and am not afraid."*
> *--Psalms 56:3-4 NIV*

God,
You know this is one of my biggest struggles. During my life, I have let worry overcome me to the point of making me ill. It made no difference in the outcome. Trusting you would have made all the difference. I believe. Please help my unbelief. Amen.

It's Just Emotion

It's emotion, I've decided. Emotion that leads to what's in the heart being spilled onto the page.

And sometimes, emotion is found to be a quiet season.

It's been that kind of season for me. I have found myself still, and occasionally, as I sit in the quiet, it doesn't even feel like I'm thinking.

Sitting quietly is a lost art. It has been beautiful. I have slowly begun to appreciate its benefits.

Mom left us at the end of February 2022. Long expected, her tired body was in need of rest, but her absence for my 61 years is still sharp.

Dad is grieving also, and some days, that's hard to watch.

Expected? Yes.

Still, it's difficult.

A long, rainy spring has brought him more downtime than I had hoped. His 84-year-old hands have been busy for a lifetime. He does not do well with idleness. His heart is better right now when he is not left in the quiet. I have done my best, along with many others, just to be there.

After a brief getaway with my husband, Covid finally caught me. Fortunately, it was a bad cold at best, but more time to sit and be quiet. My head and eyes hurt, and watching too much TV, using my phone, or reading was uncomfortable. I sat quietly. I never felt restless or alone.

THE COLLECTION

My youngest daughter will leave for New Zealand in two days with her husband, who is a native. We held a send-off party for her last night, and as I went through the motions, my heart remained steady, refusing to think about tomorrows.

Her story is unbelievable. She came to us at eight years old, somewhat like a young bird with a broken wing. She was very easy to love, and it was miraculous to watch God restore her. He did, and now those wings are ready to fly.

Meanwhile, as the calendar has continued to flip pages, I have been faithful to continue my trek through the Old Testament—not just reading but studying. As Eugene Peterson would say, it's been "A Long Obedience in the Same Direction." It's been a long but very insightful season; I've made several stops along the way but am committed to finishing.

Gathering my thoughts from the past months, we stood in church this morning to sing one of my new favorites, Graves into Gardens. The words of the chorus sank deep into my soul:

"You turn mourning to dancing

You give beauty for ashes

You turn shame into glory

You're the only one who can

You turn graves into garden

You turn bones into armies

You turn seas into highways

You're the only one who can." 6

Once again, God spoke deeply into my heart as my friend, Dave Neiss, proceeded to preach on Psalm 46, one of my favorite Psalms.

The last few months have been heart-wrenching at times, joyous at others, chaotic at others, and almost emotionless at others. One thing has been constant: My loving Father has made his presence, strength, power, and comfort obvious and available to me very clearly.

He has been my Rock.

He has been my Calm.

He was my answer before the question even entered my mind.

I look, and I see what He has done in the past.

That alone is enough for my future.

Just like the words we sang this morning:

"Oh, there's nothing better than You

There's nothing better than You

Lord, there's nothing,

Nothing is better than You."

> *"God is our refuge and strength, an ever-present help in trouble. Therefore, we will not fear, though the earth give way and the mountains fall into the heart of the sea, though its waters roar and foam and the mountains quake with their surging."--Psalms 46:1-3 NIV*

Lord, A constant comfort to our pain and a resolution to our struggles. You, Lord, meet our needs before we ask. Thank you. Amen.

Lord, Please Make It Enough

I handed my five loaves and two fish to the Lord this morning. I prayed for him to bless them and begged them to be enough.
This past fiscal year has contained many memorable moments, for which I'm grateful, but it has also found me with periods when I felt the wind knocked out of me.
The gun went off, and the marathon began when I lost Mom in February 2022.

I won't go into detail; there's been nothing monumental in the actual scheme of tragedies. It's just been a steadfast, ongoing, and relentless chaos. Sometimes, to the point, I ask, "Could we stop for a moment so I can catch my breath?" When I crawled from bed this morning to head into the day, the weight of it all hit like a hammer coming down. There's a breaking point for everybody; for me, it was this morning.
I cried tears for every event in my past year that has brought me pain. These are events that most of the world doesn't even know about. I realize that this is life, and I'm not alone.

Everyone has demons to face, challenges, frustrations, and disappointments—every day.
We all experience red lights when we are expecting green ones.
It couldn't be accomplished if I attempted to decipher this all alone. It wouldn't happen. I would find myself in more despair than now.

The one who prayed over the loaves and fish fed over 10,000 and provided 12 baskets surplus. The man who beckoned Peter to get out of the boat calmed the storm and helped him get back in the boat. The God who took on the world's sins didn't disappoint us by leaving us in our brokenness.

If I were to say, I can do this; I've got this, I would be lying.
I can't do this. But, I have the assurance that he will take what I have, bless it, and it will be enough.
I know he will never leave my side, and I'm assured that my home is with him in the present and the future.
This morning, I lift up my five loaves and two fish and ask, Lord, please make it enough.

> *"Jesus then took the loaves, gave thanks, and distributed to those who were seated as much as they wanted. He did the same with the fish. When they had all had enough to eat, he said to his disciples, "Gather the pieces that are left over. Let nothing be wasted." So they gathered them and filled twelve baskets with the pieces of the five barley loaves left over by those who had eaten."*
> *--John 6:11-13 NIV*

Yesterday, today, and tomorrow, Lord, you will meet my needs. In this promise, I trust. Thank you. Amen.

Running With Focus

The year was 2014. It was a year of reconnecting with my younger self from days gone by.
I had spent six months training to run a 10k at the Outer Banks of North Carolina. My daughter would follow the next day with her first marathon.
The day came and passed all too quickly. I finished third place in my age group, 50-59, and was pleased. I watched my daughter run an amazing marathon the next day.
The joy of the victory was short. My left retina tore two weeks later. Frightening as it was, the repair was successful, and by mid-January, I was grateful for the quality of my returned eyesight. What a comfort. The doctor told me that a subsequent cataract would likely form on that eye. It did, but it didn't happen as slowly as anticipated. Once it started to grow, I quickly lost focus in that eye. It was unbelievable how rapidly my crystal-clear vision had become blurry.
Is that not like our human nature?
We can see things clearly on some days and Sundays, but our focus on Monday transforms quickly.
Peter wasn't any different, as Matthew relays in Chapter 16 of his book. Jesus presents the question, "Who do you say I am?"
"Simon Peter answered, "You are the Messiah, the Son of the living God."
With a huge pat on the back from the God of the universe, Peter is on top of the world. Jesus follows with these words:

> *"And I tell you that you are Peter, and on this rock, I will build my church, and the gates of Hades will not overcome it." --Matthew 16:16 NIV*

It doesn't take long for Peter to forget the one who gave him sight.

"From that time on, Jesus began to explain to his disciples that he must go to Jerusalem and suffer many things at the hands of the elders, the chief priests and the teachers of the law, and that he must be killed and on the third day be raised to life."

> *"Peter took him aside and began to rebuke him. "Never, Lord!" he said. "This shall never happen to you!" --Matthew 16:21, 22, NIV*

Jesus' quick words of praise transition very fast:

> *"Jesus turned and said to Peter, "Get behind me, Satan! You are a stumbling block to me; you do not have in mind the concerns of God, but merely human concerns." --Matthew 16:21, 22, NIV*

Peter lost his focus, and it wasn't a slow fade.
That vow to be patient turns fuzzy in the rearview mirror when a co-worker frustrates us.
The promise to be more loving dissipates when our efforts aren't received graciously.
Our generosity fades when the receiver doesn't use the gift the way we intended.
The list goes on.
There is only one way to maintain clear vision.
Start each day with your eyes on the One who gives you sight.
Whether reading, singing, praying, or listening, Jesus can help you navigate through what's ahead in the day. Don't start the day blindly. He's the Breakfast of Champions!
Lord, *"May these words of my mouth and this meditation of my heart be pleasing in your sight, Lord, my Rock and my Redeemer."--Psalms 19:14 NIV*

Giants Fall Hard

The physical therapist firmly grasps the gait belt and assists him to stand. After claiming his balance, he grasps the walker and proceeds to ambulate at a shuffle. The back of his gown gapes open, revealing his bare back and undergarments.
I stand dumbfounded and reflective. My mind questions everything I know about life. Why do we arrive in this world helpless and then leave the world helpless while we fight for independence the entire time?
My brain transports me to a different place and era.
My dad hollers, "Back up a little bit. You wanted fly balls, and you're going to get them."
We inch backward, only to watch the ball sail over the top of our heads. I watched again as he picked up the baseball, swung the bat mightily, and sent the baseball soaring. Gauging myself underneath, I caught a glimpse of the sun, just long enough to misjudge the placement of my glove. I felt the sting of the ball as it pelted my thigh.
"You've got to get under it," Dad hollered. "You're not going to succeed if you're scared."
He had a way of encouraging and pushing that didn't leave you feeling condemned. His words contained prophetic wisdom I never realized until now.
Departing from my baseball memory, I find myself in the farrowing house. My sister and I scramble to catch pigs as Dad stands ready with the clippers to trim off their sharp, newborn teeth. The teeth can be threatening to the mama sow during nursing and can be a threat to each other. This was always a standard practice in our hog farming operation.
Dad always kept up with the latest trends and changes in agriculture. Whether it was livestock husbandry, row-crop farming, changes in equipment, or even changes in modes of communication, Dad

never shrunk away from a challenge. He transitioned to CB radios, Business Band receivers, and later cell phones as time progressed.

His flexibility became even more apparent in the years to come as the 80-year-old climbed the tractor, set the computer, and navigated through the field via GPS. He met his biggest test head-on as he signed up to love and care for my mom through her Alzheimer's diagnosis. He bounced back from a catastrophic hip fracture after proving he couldn't bounce.

And here we are now as he struggles daily to maintain his mobility and find a balance with his aging, declining body.

As I stand outside of his hospital room, I find myself exhausted. Another scare, another fix, and hopefully, we will go home tomorrow. I hear him address the nurse:

"I want you to know you're an excellent nurse. I've enjoyed having you take care of me and I hope I wasn't too ornery. I found out a long time ago that to get through life, you have to make it fun."

My eyes brim with tears and pride as I hear him encourage his caregiver. As a nurse, I know how far those words go.

You have made it fun, Dad. Even today, I found myself laughing at your humor and good nature.

How can it be that I enjoyed sitting with you all day at the hospital? You have always inspired me. Having watched you rise to many challenges, I will do my best not to back down.

At this point, I am frightened. That's only natural.

I still hear your words, "You're not going to succeed if you're scared." So I put away my fear and prepare to face whatever is next.

Thanks for teaching me a lifetime of lessons.

> *"Children's children are a crown to the aged, and parents are the pride of their children."--Proverbs 17:6 NIV*

Thank you, Lord, for the gift of my parents, the lessons they taught, and the legacy of faith they passed on. They have been a blessing. Amen.

Looking For the Miracle

Scrolling through social media, I absent-mindedly saw the picture: a 9-month-old hooked up to tubes and wires and monitors with pleas for prayer from the distraught mother and family. A small tumble off the couch had ended up in a horrific brain bleed just because of the way she had landed on a major artery. I would have never noticed the post other than that she resembled my youngest granddaughter. The picture unsettled me, almost making me ill. It reminded me how quickly things can change and how frail life is.

I began to pray nonstop for many days for this sweet baby. I read the updates and donated to help them with the financial burden they were going through. The odds were stacked against them. The bleed was significant, surgery was imminent, and there were warnings from neurologists about what probably lay ahead. Nine days later, she went home. The parents proudly displayed a smiling, beautiful baby girl surrounded by gifts. January 2, another picture after an excellent check-up. The miracle had happened.

So many people miss the miracles. It's not that they're not there. It's that we're not looking for them. Or do we want to explain them away with science, timing, or some other explanation our human brains can take? So sometimes we stop looking for them.

Calvary was one of those miracles. Unfortunately, many aren't looking for the miracle there. They need something their brains can wrap around. Someone being raised from the dead isn't exactly that. If you study the history of Jesus' crucifixion, you will know how much blood was poured out. Beatings after beatings and ultimately the spear in the side that allowed the blood and water to flow. The brokenness of his body from the horrific scourging, the trip up to Golgotha carrying his cross, and the effort it took to secure each breath of air as he hung suspended from his arms. He died. But yet, on the third day, the tomb was empty; he was alive, and the miracle had occurred for those of us looking for the miracle. But let me take it one step further: isn't the biggest miracle that God had already planned a way for our reconciliation through that cross?

What is mankind that you were mindful of them?
Psalm 8:4 NIV.

But yet while we were still sinners, he died for us.
Romans 5:8 NIV.

From the book of John 1:14 NIV, he was full of unfailing love and faithfulness from his abundance, and we receive one gracious blessing after another.
Yes. The miracle. He loves us so much. He chose us. He redeemed us. He suffered for us. He arose for us.
Let that miracle resonate deep in your heart today.
It's there, and it's for everybody.

"Why do you look for the living among the dead?
He is not here; he has risen! Remember how he told
you, while he was still with you in Galilee:"
--Luke 24:5-6 NIV

Lord, Thank you for the miracle of healing the nine-month-old baby. Thank you for the miracle at Calvary. Thank you for the miracle you have made in me. Amen.

Chapter 8

Mom

Chances are, if you spent time in my first book, you feel like you already know my mom. Our journey with her Alzheimer's stirred a lot of memories and reflection.

On her 85th birthday, two years after her death, I wrote this:

Today is my mom's 85th birthday, or it would have been. I know our celebrations here pale to those in her heavenly home.

For several years, I have mourned that ten years had been taken from her life by the cruel disease of Alzheimer's. Even though there is truth to that statement, I can now stand back and see the good God brought from it.

*I watched my dad emerge as a caregiver and love like I've never witnessed before. I saw his tenderness and vulnerability in a new light.

*Our family grew closer as we worked together to provide her care and love her as she so deserved.

*We had time to recognize and remember all she had been for our family, church, and community.

*My father grew closer to God and loves reading his Bible. His relationship with his Savior has grown immensely.

*My relationship with my dad is better than I had ever imagined.

*We learned that with God's help, families can journey through adversity and come out on the other side.

I wouldn't wish this on anyone, but there are moments of gratefulness throughout every storm.

Look for them.

Look for Him.

Hang on to the only anchor that is secure. You can't weather the storm without it.

Kindness Lives On

After all this time, you would think all the good stories had been handed down.

We sat at the dinner table, too full to get up and start dishes. We lingered over good conversation.

Dad had just fixed another stellar meal: steak, baked potatoes, corn on the cob, and freshly sliced tomatoes. (Next week, my store-bought chicken will pale in comparison.) My aunt, Dad's sister, had pitched in with the literal cherry on top, cherry cheesecake.

This was the Sunday routine. Dad would arrive at church in his 'Side by Side,' and my husband and I would sit 'side by side' with him through the service.

Afterward, we would head to his house for lunch. We all took turns preparing the meal. Today's after-lunch topic turned to school. It will be starting soon. A neighborhood prayer vigil would occur that night for teachers, students, and the year ahead. I reflected on one of the biggest things I had prayed for my children. I didn't pray for popularity. I prayed they might make that one true friend that would be there for them through the good and the bad.

My aunt began to share a story. I love her stories, rich in detail and usually a surprise ending.
She said she knew the feeling of needing that one friend. She had gone to a small country school for several years. Upon starting the fourth grade, she would begin at Galesburg Elementary. She shared she was scared and nervous because she didn't know anyone. Standing at the merry-go-round, she felt so alone and abandoned. A little girl came over and asked if she wanted to swing with her.
They became instant friends and would stay that way through grade school, high school, and all through life. That little girl was my mom. She married her best friend's brother, my dad.

I knew Mom's compassion and kindness as a mother, Sunday School teacher, and community member.
Tears brimmed my eyes, knowing she was already a kind human as a fourth-grader.

It's never too early to teach your kids the difference they can make in someone's life.
It's never too early to teach kindness.

> *"Be kind and compassionate to one another, forgiving each other, just as in Christ God forgave you." --Ephesians 4:32 NIV*

Heavenly Father, I memorized this scripture years ago but am still learning to live it. May I be inspired by loved ones before me who modeled kindness in their lives. Amen.

Faithfulness

The whole evening had been difficult.

Following our normal Sunday routine, I drove directly to Dad's and Mom's after work. With his growing cooking expertise, Dad had already prepared a wonderful stew for my husband and me.
As he brought Mom to the kitchen table in her wheelchair, I could see it had been a long day. She kept her eyes closed with her head resting on her hand. Occasionally, she would reach out and grip the table and try to shake it, always followed by scratching her head vigorously. Despite the meds she was receiving, her struggle seemed to be increasing.

She ate a few bites of stew I fed her, but it became difficult as she tried multiple times to bite the metal spoon. At one point, she clamped down hard, and I envisioned broken teeth to follow. My 38 years of nursing experience began with problem-solving by considering the available adaptive devices.

After we all had finished eating, it became apparent that she would only take a few bites tonight. Drinking was minimal as well, and my mind quickly began to have concerns about dehydration.
The final trip to the bathroom was mainly routine. The grabbing, shaking of the mechanical lift, and patting to my back that quickly turned to slapping indicated even more anxiousness.
At one point, I asked her, "Mom, do you feel nervous tonight?" She stopped, quieted, and sat still for a moment. She mumbled a few words unfamiliar with any language and then began shaking again.

My soul ached deeply for wherever my mom was at the moment. After we transferred her to bed, Dad returned to the kitchen to get her bedtime meds. I unhooked the mechanical lift and sat down beside her. Unsafe now to sit on the side of the bed by herself, I snuggled in close to her and put my arm around her. It was what she needed to hold herself up and what I needed to hold myself up at this moment. I needed to hold my mama.

I felt her melt into me as she leaned closer and laid her head on my shoulder. I reached over and stroked her hair and softly whispered how much I loved her and how much she meant to me. Dad took a little longer than usual to retrieve the meds and yogurt, which would be the vehicle to get the meds down. Somehow, he knew.

I was glad he took his time.

For that moment, it was peaceful and quiet; the demons stood back and left her alone as she lay against my shoulder. Time stood still.

After the meds, we tucked her in, and she settled into a deep sleep. Her face looked angelic and sweet, the face I remembered as my mama.

My dad is amazing. I don't know how long we've been on this journey now, and I don't care to try to remember. It's taken lots of extra hands, outside resources, and adaptive methods of doing things, but mostly, it's taken so much of my Dad.

He is still vibrant and can talk you under the table, but he's tired.

He's worn.

He's weary.

I love them both so much. He made a vow almost 63 years ago, and that vow got serious when this disease got serious.

There's only one explainable reason why he's remained so strong.

And that was his first vow before he knew my mama—his vow to Jesus. Neither is perfect, but they have spent a lifetime pursuing the One who is. My parents have been faithful beyond the definition of the word. Stuck in my human ways, all I can do is rejoice that I know that faithfulness. It's what Jesus has for me every moment of every day.

And because of that great faithfulness, we will weather this storm and come out on the other side.

Yes, great is thy faithfulness,

Morning by morning,

New mercies, I see.

All I have needed
thy hand hath provided.
Great is thy faithfulness
God unto me. ~Thomas O. Chisholm 1923

If you have been down this road, I'm sure you understand. If you have not, I am sure you know someone who has.

In amongst the tragic way we are losing my mom, I want to be able to look back someday and remember the moments that I will always cherish. *We lost Mom on February 28, 2022, just months after I wrote this. It was a bittersweet blessing as we watched her slip into the arms of Jesus. I'm thankful for such a wonderful mom, but I would never know my dad as I do without this journey. Thank you, Lord, for never leaving us on the broken road. Amen.

Waiting and Trusting

I was reminded today of this verse:

> *"As the rain and the snow come down from heaven, and do not return to it without watering the earth and making it bud and flourish, so that it yields seed for the sower and bread for the eater, so is my word that goes out from my mouth: It will not return to me empty, but will accomplish what I desire and achieve the purpose for which I sent it." --Isaiah 55:10-11 NIV*

As I sit and reflect on my visit last night with Mom, now reaching the latter stages of Alzheimer's, the hollow look in her eyes can be haunting. Even my Thesaurus cannot find a better word.
I do ashamedly stand and dare to question God.
My head hangs as my thoughts spill to him that no one else can hear.
Is this what the devoted, dedicated woman had to look forward to?
Is this what teaching almost 30 years of Sunday School reaps?
Is this what selflessly giving of yourself for years to your family, kids, and grandkids results in?
Cooking, cleaning, loving, serving, forgiving, and always encouraging. And here she sits. As I try to converse, I know my words fall on ears that hear but do not understand.
Even my hugs and kisses are sometimes pushed or swatted away.
We've reached the point that even a soft human touch can threaten her.

I know my mom's life has been more productive than most, and has pointed to him and given Him glory for most of her life. Every hug passed out in Sunday school, every donut retrieved, every story listened to, and every story she, in turn, told, does not go out and return void.

I know He has and will continue to do everything He has planned.
I know her future is bright.
I know entirely, without a doubt, where she's going and where she will spend eternity.
It is in the here and now, at this point, that I struggle the most.
We mourned when we got the diagnosis.
We mourned at each step when another facet of my mom was taken away.
And we will mourn when she leaves this earth.
Even though we celebrate where she's going, right now, all I see is where she is, and most of the time, I don't know where that is.
That's the part I have to be honest about because I don't understand.
I do understand she's not going to be healed, but yet I can't uncurl my fingers around her long enough to let go and pray that He takes her home.
So, we sit and wait.

We speak soothing words to her as I try to be my dad's biggest cheerleader.
I will continue to approach her slowly as if approaching a deer or any other scared creature.
With every pat, hug, and kiss, I will be grateful for every time she smiles.
I will be grateful every time she eats a good meal, and I will be thankful for the occasional time she'll reach out and hug me.
More than anything, I will be grateful for what God has sent out; I know it will not return void.
Yes, I know.
And I will trust.

> *"So is my word that goes out from my mouth: It will not return to me empty, but will accomplish what I desire and achieve the purpose for which I sent it."*
> *--Isaiah 55:11 NIV*

God, My mother's faithfulness touched so many lives, but the biggest one was mine. Thank you. Amen.

His Visit

The corn is picked, the beans are harvested and in the bins, and the farmers are frantically getting the last batches of wheat planted.

Winter is on the horizon.

I sat in my parent's living room, the afternoon sun streaming through the window as I watched my mom wrestle with her blanket. She reclined in her lift chair as I prayed she might find a peaceful afternoon nap. Most of my efforts of affection today had been deflected. Sometimes, I fear she is losing her eyesight as her soft blue eyes stare hollowly at me. When I catch her looking at something across the room, I realize it's not her eyesight that she is losing.

Despite these descriptions, it has been a pleasant Sunday.

Dad watched most of the church service on YouTube and then insisted on fixing steaks for us for lunch. A nice conversation accompanied our meal.

Just as we were leaving, an elder from our church came to visit.

Visits, unfortunately, are few and far between, but as I sat in the corner and observed, I felt a bit invisible, like the fly on the wall taking in the conversation.

Both men had shown great longevity in their walk with Jesus and remained steadfast. Both have served on the church board as elders for many years. They have spent years, under God's direction, making many decisions for the future of our church.

And so, they visited.

My heart swelled with admiration for these two giants as I listened in.

Dad sat beside his frail, feeble partner of 63 years and occasionally reached out and patted her arm. The view was humbling as he visited and still directed his attention to what was once a vibrant woman of dedicated service to her church and family.

Our visitor sat across the room and took in the sadness of the scene.

It is comparable to the sadness reflected in his own eyes. Not quite a year past, this servant had lost his lifetime mate of over 50 years. He speaks of the challenges he now faces without the partner he shared life with for so long. Just having finished Thanksgiving, his comments were, "I got through it." Knowing that Christmas was not too far ahead, his children had already started planning ways to navigate through and keep last year's precious memories intact.

My husband and I sat for a short while before politely exiting and allowing them to visit.
They have so much in common, yet so vastly different.

Both men, pillars of faith, raised their families in the church and had always put God at the top of the list and the family next.

Here they are now, at one of the hardest legs of the journey. Neither knew twenty years ago that this would be where they would be now. That knowledge would not have changed a thing.

Their decision to sign on the dotted line, whether to follow Christ or at the bottom of the marriage certificate, was a decision to remain faithful to the end. They took the covenant seriously.

The hardship they both now encounter is endured and tolerated with a deep sense of faith. Their lifelong dedication is just as strong now as when they started.

THE COLLECTION

They both knew that just because you're a follower of Christ, your life will never be free of hardship.

It's Who you travel with that brings about all the difference.

My view from the corner has been bittersweet and encouraging. They continue to fight the good fight and point to Jesus in everything they do.

Even though they love life and their families, they both look ahead to heaven, to being home again, whole, and in no more pain. More than anything, they look to the day of being in the presence of the glory of God.

What an honor to have witnessed a small glimpse of this visit.

What an honor to have witnessed their lives.

> *"Gray hair is a crown of splendor; it is attained*
> *in the way of righteousness."*
> *--Proverbs 16:31 NIV*

Lord, Thank you for these two living examples of faithfulness, love, and endurance. May I learn from them. Amen.

One Last Lesson From Mom

Our last hurrah.
That's what I'm calling it.
I thought a change in medication brought on two weeks of increased clarity, smiles, and even verbal expression.
I believe it was God's way of giving us one last treasured memory from the woman who made and shaped my family. She kissed me six times that night and told me she loved me.
As we sat posed for the picture, Dean asked if I was ready. I said as soon as my eyes cleared.

I'm too exhausted right now to express all the gratitude I have for my family, the way we worked together those last days, and the way we loved and laughed as we celebrated her life and laid her to rest. The way my kids came alongside me and carried me through the week. I am the wealthiest woman in the world.
I have no words to express my overflowing gratitude to the three giants who preached at her funeral and testified to a life that glorified God, even at the end.
I have no words for my friends, community, and church family, who have gone above and beyond to love, care, and support my family.
Life is hard. Life is sometimes not fair. But in the end, God is always good, and His plans and purposes are sovereign. Family is priceless, and community and friends are invaluable. Don't waste time on petty small stuff because, in the end, we only need two things in life: God and each other.

> *"He has shown you, O mortal, what is good. And what does the Lord require of you? To act justly and to love mercy and to walk humbly with your God."*
> *--Micah 6:8 NIV*

Lord, Your kindness and goodness were so easily seen in the last days we shared with Mom. We were blessed, and we are grateful. Amen.

Mom's Last Goodbye

It was the most vulnerable state I had ever seen him in. I stood beside his bed as he struggled for words to answer my questions.
The last four days had been spent at Mom's bedside. We had marveled that we still had her after three years of Hospice care, but it was obvious her Alzheimer's was closing in, and it wouldn't be long now. She had fought hard all day despite the Hospice comfort meds. My niece and I had just said goodbye to a roomful of relatives and were getting ready to settle in for a long night. I had asked her to stay because I sensed the time was near. I went in to brush my teeth, and a thought struck me, "Maybe she's waiting to hear from Dad one last time."
I went back into her room only to hear my niece ask me, "Do you think she's waiting on Grandpa to tell her goodbye?" Goosebumps emerged in our synchronized thoughts.

This is what placed me at his bedside. With his understanding and agreement, he had moved to the adjacent room to sleep so we could be better attentive to Mom throughout the night.
"Dad," I hesitantly woke him. "I'm sure tonight is going to be the night. Have you told her goodbye? I feel like she's waiting on something."
Seeing the stress and pain on his face was comparable to the pain next door as Mom struggled.

Softly, he answered, "I've told her goodbye. I kissed her on the forehead. I gave her permission to go. I'll go back in if you think I need to, but it's almost more than I can handle."
Looking at this eighty-three-year-old man who had given his all the past ten years for her care, I saw that part of him was dying alongside her.

"I don't have words to tell you how much I love this woman," he continued.
Such a poetic sentence coming from this long time farmer's mouth.
"I've told her I love her every day and even more since she's been sick. I'll go back in if I need to; it's just…"
I stopped him.
"No, Dad. As long as you're okay, I'm okay."
I couldn't bear to put him through anymore, and I couldn't bear to lose both of them at once.
I told him we would wake him if anything changed.
As I went back into Mom's room, I asked my niece if she had heard my Dad.
"I heard everything," she said.
That seemed a bit amiss since it was in the room next door, but maybe it was because the house seemed extra quiet.
I noticed at that point that my mom's breathing had changed. The wet-sounding respirations were gone. They had slowed.
I leaned over and kissed my mom on the forehead, and stroked her hair. "I know you heard Dad. He loves you more than he has words to describe. That's how we all feel about you, too. You have been the best wife, mom, and grandma. You've given more than we could've ever asked for. You can go meet Jesus now. He's waiting."

The last four respirations were slow and spaced.
It was over. Just like that.
My mom loved my dad fiercely. She loved all of us with every part of her being. She was waiting for one last time to hear Dad say how much he loved her.
And then she went.
She went into the arms of a Love that there are no words to describe. I am incapable of knowing how wide and long and high and deep that love is.
My Mom isn't.

> *"And I pray that you, being rooted and established in love, may have power, together with all the Lord's holy people, to grasp how wide and long and high and deep is the love of Christ,*

*and to know this love that surpasses knowledge—that you
may be filled to the measure of all the fullness of God."
-- Ephesians 3:17-19 NIV*

Lord, You allowed me the greatest privilege ever–to help walk my mom into your arms. Thank you for that bittersweet memory I will always cherish. Amen

Heaven

My latest Bible study brought me to the table this morning with Jesus. The conversation was about death. We covered as much as we could with what the author had written, what God had written, and as far as my thoughts could take me.

My thoughts continued as the study invariably challenged me with questions.

I began reflecting on what heaven might look like as far as I could imagine.

Just two and a half months ago, my mama had left this earth for her heavenly home. I began to let my thoughts roam.

What does her day look like? But wait, does she have a day/night? Scripture reveals:

> *"But do not forget this one thing, dear friends: With the Lord a day is like a thousand years, and a thousand years are like a day."*
> *--2 Peter 3:8 NIV*

Our world is divided into 24-hour segments. Hypothetically, what could she do 24 hours a day without sleeping, resting, and eating? But technically, there probably aren't 24 hours in a day in heaven, and I realized my brain would explode if I tried to figure this out. On earth:

A warm embrace from a loved one fills an empty spot in the soul. Does she experience that?

Words of encouragement and affirmation allow my spirit to soar. Does that happen in heaven?

Lying on a soft mattress under a pile of luxurious fluffy blankets lets me close my eyes and relax. Does she need that?

A perfectly cooked steak with a loaded baked potato on the side brings immeasurable pleasure and satisfaction. Does she desire that?

The scent of an iris, the aroma of warm baked bread, or the smell of a fresh spring rain floods my soul with memories. Does she remember me?

A shopping trip with a friend for a few fine purchases releases dopamine into my system and fulfills a longing. Is the joy she experiences so different?

Exercise releases endorphins, which give me a sense of well-being and contentment. Does that exist for her continuously?

Intimacy with my partner instills connectivity, gratefulness, and fulfillment. Does she miss my dad?

A day with grandkids makes my heart happy and my face smile. Is that type of joy experienced in other ways?

Comparing heaven to earth is ludicrous. It's impossible.

It's useless.

It's senseless.

Here's what I know:

"The Lord will rescue me from every evil attack and will bring me safely to his heavenly kingdom. To him be glory for ever and ever. Amen."
--2 Timothy 4:18 NIV

> *"For we know that if the earthly tent we live in is destroyed, we have a building from God, an eternal house in heaven, not built by human hands."*
> *--2 Corinthians 5:1 NIV*

> *"But our citizenship is in heaven. And we eagerly await a Savior from there, the Lord Jesus Christ," --Philippians 3:20 NIV*

> *"Whom have I in heaven but you? And earth has nothing I desire besides you." --Psalms 73:25 NIV*

> *"'He will wipe every tear from their eyes. There will be no more death' or mourning or crying or pain, for the old order of things has passed away."*
> *--Revelation 21:4 NIV*

Earthly hugs, relationships, food, shopping trips, family gatherings, material things, and experiences on this great earth are true blessings. Intertwined amongst those are illnesses, car wrecks, bankruptcy, loneliness, crime, hate, and evil.

I can't begin to know exactly what heaven will be like, but I know the latter part of the abovementioned list will not exist there.

I don't want to fear death.

I don't think that I do.

I know that anywhere that Jesus is, we are going to be complete.

We are going to be more than okay. That will have to be enough for now.

> *"Praise be to the God and Father of our Lord Jesus Christ, who has blessed us in the heavenly realms with every spiritual blessing in Christ."*
> *--Ephesians 1:3 NIV*

Transitions

She lay curled up in a comfortable, sleepy daze. She rested as close as she possibly could to her mother and yet remained two separate beings. She hears her mother's heartbeat and her voice in the distance. She is safe and warm and has no desire ever to leave this place.

It won't be long until conditions become crowded and things change. In no time at all, she is pushed through a small passage and whisked into a cold, bright room, and her world transitions—a world of beautiful colors, sounds, music, love, relationships, and celebrations. Sights, smells, things to touch, taste, and emotions to feel. She finds herself connected to many heartbeats. Life, as she knows, isn't always perfect, but she has no desire ever to leave this place.

Yet, the day comes, and she transitions to another home.
It is by far the best place she has ever known.
Given the choice, she would've stayed at her first home forever, but it was never meant to be sustainable for long.
Given the choice, she would've chosen to stay at her second home. Despite the pain and chaos, she loved it, but each day soon became more challenging as she felt her outward shell wearing out.

And now she is home, truly home. This is where she was meant to be. This is where she was meant to spend all eternity.
She was meant to be beside her Creator, who gave everything so she could be there.
His heartbeat is all too familiar and by far the most comforting of all. And here, she will stay forever.

"He has made everything beautiful in its time. He has also set eternity in the human heart; yet no one can fathom what God has done from beginning to end." --Ecclesiastes 3:11 NIV

"For God so loved the world that he gave his one and only Son, that whoever believes in him shall not perish but have eternal life." --John 3:16 NIV

Father God, Oh, the things we do not know and do not understand that you have prepared for us.
We look forward to the day we shall see you face to face and spend eternity in your glory. Amen.

Enjoy The Best Mother's Day

Two months after Mom's passing, I ventured to Walmart with a two and four-year-old.
I explained that Sunday was Mother's Day, and we would celebrate our moms. Our mission was to pick out some flowers to plant for them, and we would use our new gardening set. They appeared less than enthused.
Somehow, our conversation proceeded to my mom. I explained that she didn't live here anymore and that she was in heaven.
My two-year-old granddaughter took it from there. She then reminded me that my mom's name is Gramma Mary Jo.
"She's not sick anymore."
I knew she had heard that before, but her next statement stunned me.
"She can talk now."
I don't know if someone had told her that at some point, but at any rate, it's been over two months since she left.
What a detail to be reminded of from a two-year-old.
My mom will have the best Mother's Day ever because she is whole, healthy, and yes, she can talk again!! What a celebration.

> *"But our citizenship is in heaven. And we eagerly await a Savior from there, the Lord Jesus Christ, who, by the power that enables him to bring everything under his control, will transform our lowly bodies so that they will be like his glorious body." --Philippians 3:20-21 NIV*

Thank you, Lord, for the comforting promise that my mom is with you now, and she is complete. Such a thought allows me to celebrate as well. Amen.

Mom's Durango

I've been driving a 2008 Durango for several years now.
It belonged to my mom and was the last vehicle she ever drove. She passed away in February, and we purchased a new car in August. I justified keeping the Durango because we would use it to haul things to our free store ministry, and I would need it if I ever had a car full of grandkids to transport.
It all seemed justifiable.
In the past five months, I have driven the vehicle twice. It has been parked in the shed as we continued to pay insurance, tags, and taxes.
I realized how silly that was.
I struggled with the decision.
I realized it was time to let go.

It was the last thing I remember Mom using before Alzheimer's took over.
It was the last thing I had of hers.
It was the last thing I had of Mom's.

After my pity party and a finished episode of Hoarders, I quickly realized how untrue that was.
I have Mom's smile and her cheeks.
I have her punny-ness and sense of humor.
I have Mom's stature.
I have her love of children.
I have her recipes even though I'll never cook like her.
I have Mom's compassion.
I have her sensitivity.
I have Mom's grandchildren as my children and her great-grandchildren as my grandchildren.
I have her memories.

I have her blood coursing through my veins and her love of Jesus deep within.

This.

This is so much more than a 2008 Durango.

I have her heart. 🖤

> *"Do not store up for yourselves treasures on earth, where moths and vermin destroy, and where thieves break in and steal. But store up for yourselves treasures in heaven, where moths and vermin do not destroy, and where thieves do not break in and steal. For where your treasure is, there your heart will be also." --Matthew 6:19-21 NIV*

Lord, what a treasure my mom was. Thank you for the legacy she left in me. May I be worthy of passing it on. Amen.

CHAPTER 9

Inspired

What exactly does the word inspired mean? Without going to a reputable source, I will explain what it means to me.

Inspired: to have something monumental, impactful, and moving breathed into me to the point that it affects my thoughts and actions. (brought to you by Rhondapedia. You're welcome.)
There are multiple ways to be inspired. God does it in his book, his sunrises, the birth of a baby, and the list is endless. Music, poems, and writings are inspiring.

One of the greatest inspirations in this world is our fellow man. I witness it in kindness, compassion, creativity, resiliency, and long-suffering. Multiple examples are waiting each day if we just look for them. Sometimes, they don't require us to search—they're just there. Seeing them is one thing. The goal is to let them positively affect your life. Don't stop at just being moved. Let them move you.

Sunglasses and Transistors

I sat down to do my early morning Bible study but found myself fighting with a trivial distraction. My morning routine usually finds me packing my things for the day before I head to the backroom to study. Today I could not find my new sunglasses.
I love my new sunglasses.
I don't tolerate the sun well, and because I wear glasses, I have to wear the kind that fits over them. I disliked every pair I had ever owned until last week.

These are polarized and cute, and I don't look like I need a seeing-eye dog when I wear them.
Nevertheless, I'm ashamed to admit I was having trouble focusing on God because I was focusing on sunglasses.
I began to think about another material item I had treasured, even more so than my new sunglasses. It was from long ago.
Unfortunately, my memory of what happened yesterday is not nearly as sharp as my memory from over 50 years ago.
Those details are quite clear.

It was late spring, and my mom was getting ready to take me to our local grade school for Head Start orientation. Kindergarten was not deemed necessary during the Dinosaur era, so to prepare for first grade, we would spend a few summer weeks in Head Start.
I had turned six a couple of months earlier and had received the best birthday present ever: a transistor radio. Google if you must.
I loved music, and it was pure magic to hold nonstop songs in the palm of my hands and even make choices by changing the station dial. It was a small black radio in a soft leather case with small holes. To me, it looked like an ice cream sandwich. I loved everything about that little radio.

I had asked if I could take it to the orientation. I'm unsure why my six-year-old brain thought that was a good idea. Was I going to play music for the other kids while we listened to what our next few weeks would be like? Was I going to show it off in the car to the friend who was riding with us? I don't remember my reason. But I do remember my disobedience.

My mother had said no, so I set out to devise a plan. I would need an accomplice: my sister.

I had asked her to take the radio and put it in the backseat of the car. She was 4 1/2 at the time and shorter than me. (Those days are gone.) Being the "eager-to-please" sister, she headed out on her mission. This is where my "head start" in life lessons began.

I got into the car and eagerly went to find my radio. I spent the entirety of the 5-mile drive searching on the floorboard, in the seats, between the seats, and everywhere I could fathom she might have placed it. I was frantic. The radio wasn't in the car.

I remember very little about the orientation that day other than an activity coloring a bumblebee. I colored as hard as I could with my yellow crayon as I fretted about the whereabouts of my radio.

Returning home, I inquired immediately with my sister. She explained that she had not been able to get the car door open, so she had laid the radio on the top of the trunk. Neither my mom nor I had seen it. The rest is history.

I was finally able to confess to my mom what had happened. I didn't get the lashing I had expected. I received a gentle scolding, and then we spent the next few hours driving up and down the road looking for my treasure. It was gone.

My parents were kind enough to replace the radio.

It did not have a soft black case; it was hard plastic.

It was not black. It was turquoise. It didn't look like an ice cream sandwich.

I loved it regardless.

I loved their mercy.

This was my first lesson in trusting that my mom knew what was best for me, my first lesson in learning that disobedience has consequences. It was a hard lesson for a six-year-old to learn, but one that obviously left an impression.

There wasn't any disobedience with me losing my new sunglasses this morning, just forgetfulness and they will probably turn up.

I am thankful, though, for the reminder of that first lesson in grace that came from my parents.

I would like to say that was the last time I exhibited disobedience in my life, but we all know better.

Disobedience comes in all shapes and sizes, from the big, premeditated gems to the little ones that we like to color gray. It can involve stretching the truth a bit, answering incorrectly to avoid hurting feelings, sharing a tidbit of gossip to help solve a problem that is not even ours to solve, and many others.

Nonetheless, every day we have choices in front of us that we must choose to obey what God says is best for us. In fact, there really aren't gray areas when it comes to obedience. It's black and white, just like that transistor radio.

I sure miss that radio. I loved it so much that I imagine I would still be using it today if it had not been just AM.

A lot has changed in our world.

But thank God He never will change and neither will His expectations of us either.

I'm thankful *"The Lord is merciful and compassionate, slow to get angry and filled with unfailing love."*

Wonder what happened to that radio…

More importantly, where are those sunglasses?

Thank you, Lord, for lessons that are never forgotten and for the love and mercy you give me every day. Amen.

Never Too Late to Shine

We finished loading the last two boxes of donations for the Orange Swan Free Store. I turned and looked at the house one more time. This was where Dan lived and where his story took place.

I met Dan about ten years earlier. I also met Dan about 20 years ago. Confused? You should've seen the expression on my face.

Twenty years ago, my nursing career brought me to a medical treatment center to work. Generally, our patients didn't drive themselves home after treatments but would rely on friends and family for transportation. We became close (or not) to some of those providing transportation.

One of the sweetest patients I remember had transportation awaiting, which left us all scrambling to the backroom in avoidance. Let's call this lovely lady Kay. Thin, soft-spoken, graceful, poised, and educated were just a few words to describe her. We loved caring for her and would linger at her station to share conversations.

Her husband lacked those adjectives. Gruff, aloof, domineering, grumpy, and quite possibly mad at the world was the best way to describe him. He seriously made me nervous, and I wondered what I might have done to get on his wrong side. Thus, the games of "pick a number" or "whose turn is it anyway" began. We all had to take our turn with Dan. We tried all the tricks to schmooze him, connect with him, be overly kind, etc. He was onto us.

You can't tame a wild beast when fear is pungent in the air.

Fast forward ten years. I sat in my hairdresser's chair and waited for my gray remover to process. Enough said.

Through the door bounded a cheerful, jolly, conversational man. He was a little plump, but with his round, kind face, add a beard, red

Santa suit, and voila. My memory nudged me, telling me I should know him, but I nudged back, sure that I didn't.
He visited with my hairdresser and talked about bowling, the senior center, what he was having for supper, and how much he had enjoyed church last Sunday. I couldn't stand it any longer. When he slipped to the backroom to get a cup of coffee, I asked Lynn who he was.

She explained that he rented a house from them. He was all alone now as his wife had passed from a disease she had fought for a long time. I had the puzzle framed and slowly began putting in the missing pieces.

That was Dan. No way!

I sat quietly in the chair and listened to them continue to visit. Before Lynn finished my hair, he bid her goodbye, pecked her on the cheek, and walked out the door.

"What happened to him? I knew him. I took care of his wife. We were–uh, he just wasn't our favorite. That's not him. What happened?"

She told me her unbelievable story.
Not long after Kay passed, my Bible-toting beautician friend introduced Dan to Jesus.
Not just church. Not just Jesus' words but Jesus.
Jesus' love.
She cooked for him, made appointments for him, helped clean his house, bought groceries, and put in his hearing aid batteries.

She went to church with him. She adopted him, but more than anything, she loved him.

Jesus did the rest.

I learned a long time ago that I can't change a heart. Lynn knew that, too. But thank goodness we both know the one who can.

Only Jesus can change a heart.

What a lovely job he did with Dan.

> *"I will give you a new heart and put a new spirit in you; I will remove from you your heart of stone and give you a heart of flesh." --Ezekiel 36:26 NIV*

Dear Jesus, I have thought I could change a person's heart before, and I have found myself giving you advice on how to make that happen—only you, Lord. Only you can change a heart. Please change mine. Amen.

Marlene

I hated to try again, but with the house supervisor tied up, I had no choice. IV sticks in small children were not my specialty.
I said a quick prayer, placed the tourniquet on the tiny little arm, took a deep breath, and guided the needle into the vein successfully. Her mom stood faithfully by her side, stroking her hair and comforting her with soothing words. Marlene.
You could always see Marlene coming; even if she was a block away, you knew it was Marlene. Fuchsia.
She loved fuchsia.
I'm assuming she loved it: Fuchsia lipstick, fuchsia tennis shoes, fuchsia jacket, fuchsia purse, fuchsia accessories. If it comes in fuchsia, she owned it.
I began to think of her as the pink lady.
Even though she wasn't a volunteer at the hospital, she was a frequent flier. Before, there was a ribbon of every color for every disease to wear on our sleeve to show support; there was Marlene—and Fuschia. You're familiar with the ribbons: pink for breast cancer, yellow for osteosarcoma, green for brain injury, purple for Alzheimer's, etc. I don't know what Marlene stood for. As peculiar as it appeared, I envisioned my wardrobe with multiples of the same color. What color would I pick?
Back to the IV, I helped secure the tubing and the arm to a supporting splint board.
"The lab tests will be back soon; hopefully, the doctor will be in after that. Do you need anything?"
"No, we're fine," was all she answered.
Marlene was always by herself during these hospital visits. She was never accompanied by the father of this child, never accompanied by another sibling. I didn't know her story outside of these walls.

What I did know was Marlene's child was chronically ill. With each returning visit, Marlene had most likely found a new purse or pair of shoes that matched her collection.

I've always had a weakness for attempting to fill in the blanks of the rest of the story I didn't know.

Right now, all I know is a lot I didn't know. How did she handle the pressure of having a chronically ill child? I don't know if this child will ever outgrow this condition. I don't know if this child will eventually grow up, graduate high school, get a job, get married, or wear Fuschia. What I do know: Marlene is here, she is faithful, she isn't shaken, she is a rock for her child, and she is dressed in fuchsia.

Maybe in a world where everything appears black and white, Marlene only wished to bring some color into her child's life.

It is fascinating that I met Marlene in 1983 while working at a small hospital in southeast Kansas. That would be 41 years ago. Her name wasn't Marlene. I don't remember her name.

There is still a lot I do remember. I still remember her love and dedication to her child and the color she brought into whatever situation she entered.

I hope and pray that my life will be remembered for something that vibrant. Wherever I go, whatever I do, whatever lives I influence, may I leave them with the warmth of bright color, just like Marlene did. She got my attention. I will never forget her.

> *"Follow God's exam, therefore, as dearly loved children and walk in the way of love, just as Christ loved us and gave himself up for us as a fragrant offering and sacrifice to God."* --Ephesians5:1-2 NIV

Lord, Some people leave a mark in our lives that lasts for a lifetime. May I influence others in positive ways for your Kingdom. Amen.

Live Love

A quick search reveals this as an Orange day lily or Tiger Lily. If you're a botanist or avid flower lover, you may correct me if needed. I'm sure your grandmother had another name for them. I've called them Corn Lilies for years, and it appears they are not.

These flowers are quickly becoming my favorite among the domestic varieties. I've always loved them.

My maternal grandmother had two long rows in her front yard, making a vast corridor. This area in her yard became our pretend playhouse of lilies, lilac bushes, roses, and irises. We could spend hours out there, our imaginations running wild.

I now have my own transplanted row s in my backyard, gifted by my aunt. They follow the sun throughout the day.

What I've noticed about these flowers is that they are indiscriminate in where they grow. Frequently, I spot them in ditches amongst overgrown grass and weeds. They may be seen amongst brush and trees or in the middle of a junk pile. Their little pop of color adds beauty to an area that is just not pretty. It would be downright ugly if it weren't for the flowers chosen to shine there. Their only requirement seems to be an ample supply of sun exposure.

Going on for several years now, I surmise we are being played. Look back over the past 3-4 years at least. Incident after incident has arisen. Each time, conflicting events have split us.
Everything is either black or white. Every topic has a line drawn down the middle: do/don't, yes/no, hate/love. Respect for each other is gone. Teeth are clenched, fists are shaking, and our opinion is the only right one. The father of lies sits back, folds his arms, and laughs maniacally.

I scrolled through my phone last night. It was exhausting. My first reaction? Give up Facebook, live your life, and love your God. But I'm not giving up that easily.

I want to be just like these flowers. I desire to be a bright spot and a glimpse of beauty amid the ugly. I want to live love in the midst of a world that is hurting, confused, and striking out.

As I scrolled through Facebook tonight, I resolved to look for the flowers. Many of you are just that. I love you for it. Your family pictures make me smile. I identify with your struggles, which are similar to mine. Your corny dad jokes distract me. Your love for your pets warms my heart. Your prayer requests make me pray. Your losses have become mine. You love me despite differences, and I love you. You are a light in my world.

This world will never be ideal because it's not our permanent home, but we have choices. The biggest one is, do we live love or do we live hate? You're the only one who can answer that.

Be a flower in the middle of the junk.

> *"If I could speak all the languages of earth and of angels, but didn't love others, I would only be a noisy gong or a clanging cymbal. Three things will last forever—faith, hope, and love—and the greatest of these is love."*
> *--1 Corinthians 13:1, 13 NLT*

Father God, May I love my neighbor as myself and treat others in the same manner I want to be treated. Lord, help me to live love. Amen.

Thoughts of an Old Testament Journey

I started on a mission a while back. I continue to wade through the Old Testament slowly. At times, I am drawn to my view of our Father Almighty. At other moments, I am horrified by the violence that I have and continue to witness; my jaw drops at the corruption as God's people continue to return to the vomit they had left behind. And I'm only in 2nd Samuel.

King David, the shepherd boy David, is often called a "man after God's own heart." I recognize his good qualities, but being the human I am, I get stuck on his faults and frailties. Not yet to the story of his adultery with Bathsheba, I have witnessed so many acts of violence and taking of wives that I cannot quite understand. Even though I know the ending, part of me wonders if, at some point, the scales will tip in the other direction, and he will have crossed the line just a bit too far.

God had a mission for David. His family would be the lineage that brought forth the Messiah, the supreme sacrifice for our sins.

God knew the mistakes David would make but saw a heart we could only glimpse into. He never gave up on David and his purpose. David suffered many consequences for his sins, but he also accomplished what God had in mind for him.

God doesn't give up on those He has called. So unlike us at times. Though not always the case, I have witnessed Christians many times shooting their wounded, giving up because they tipped our human scales one microscopic bit too far.

What do we know about a man's heart? We only truly understand our own; daily reflection is required to stay focused and unadulterated.
Each of us has a mission—many of us have several. We're going to make mistakes along the way, and some of those mistakes will have heavy consequences.
Despite the hope of a happily ever after on this earth, that will have to wait until we gather with the saints around the throne.
May I be found to encourage and not enable.
May I strive to be compassionate and not hateful.
May I be described as loving and not legalistic.
May I never water down God's truth and sanctity. May I never find my hands picking up *stones* when they could be used to help pick up *someone*. No one truly knows my heart but God. May he find me someone after His own.

> *"Search me, God, and know my heart; test me and know my anxious thoughts. See if there is any offensive way in me, and lead me in the way everlasting."*
> *--Psalms 139:23-24 NIV*

Lord, thank you for leading me to the Old Testament and the lessons contained within. May I listen and learn. Amen.

The Shop Rag

I sat on the bed and reached into my bag to retrieve the last of my packed items. What I thought was a washcloth turned out to be a gray shop rag.
I retraced my steps to the origin of this rag and how it had ended up in my possession. An unlikely source, or so it had seemed, had given it to me with words that brought tears to my eyes.
I was honored.
Following a sermon about Jesus and the famous foot washing, each congregation member was given a challenge and a shop rag.
Maybe I didn't fully get the jist of my gifter's words, but I felt like I had just been picked as one of the twelve.
His challenge had been to find someone who had modeled servanthood and give them the shop rag. He handed it to me. It would also serve as a reminder to continue in service and that we are all called to follow in His steps steadfastly.
I have been taking the rag to work and setting it next to my computer, taking it to the free store as I work on donations, and taking it to Dad's as I continue to help him get back on his feet. I forgot I had packed it this morning when I returned to his house for several days.

I stood looking at the rag. I clutched it to my chest. Today was one of those days I needed the reminder. The reminder of all those verses I have read, studied, and memorized all my life. The big one was the reminder of why we are here in the first place.

> "Instead, whoever wants to become great among you must be your servant, and whoever wants to be first must be servant of all. For even the Son of Man did not come to be served, but to serve, and to give his life as a ransom for many."
> --Mark 10:43-45 NIV

THE COLLECTION

Who would have thought such a simple rag could bring about such a reminder?
A reminder to get back in the game.
Hold your chin up.
Rely on strength that's not of your own.
Love like you have watched Him love, and remember that sometimes love requires sacrifice.
It doesn't need to be wrapped in a red bow because it is always the greatest gift you can give.
Many times, it's the hardest thing you will ever do.

Lord, Please don't ever let me forget the many acts of service you performed for others. I want to follow your example. Amen.

Stand Up

The view was amazing. We sat at a counter facing a huge window overlooking the marina. Outside, families in jackets prepared to board their rented pontoon boats for a day of adventure. That adventure seemed sketchy at best as the temperature hovered at 52 degrees.

We sat and enjoyed our Chai and bagels as I tapped my leg nervously. Our reservations were approximately an hour and a half away. The reservations were to paddleboard across the lake, which, for the life of me, I couldn't figure out why. The lake surely had to be frozen, right? Ok, honestly, it had been my idea for my daughter and me to try stand-up paddle boarding, better known as SUP.

Let me be upfront with you.

I'm not afraid of water. Well, not drastically, at least.

I'm not afraid of new challenges. Well, for the most part.

I'm not afraid of adventure. Well, as long as I know what to expect.

But I am afraid of hypothermia, aka being uncomfortable.

If people were boarding boats with coats and blankets, what would it feel like to stand up on a flotation device in a swimming suit over a body of water at 52 degrees?

As we climbed back into the car to head to the outfitter, I feigned a possible back injury. She didn't bite.

Then, I began to explain how vulnerable I might be to infection if I were to get too cold for too long. After all, I was 60.

She wasn't biting.

She was pushing me. I didn't want to be pushed, but I didn't want to disappoint her.

She was pushing me to go outside of my comfort level.

Pushing me to try something new.

Pushing me to pursue the adventure.

Pushing me to go through with what I had started.

So, what actually could be the cost of my failure?
What could be the worst-case scenario?
That I fall into some freezing water, have my breath taken away for a second, climb back up, and laugh myself silly?
I took a deep breath and climbed out of the car.
Two short hours later, we returned. The sun had come out; it was a beautiful day. We had easily mastered the board and found it exhilarating, relaxing, and with stunning views. We laughed as we headed to the car. How sad it would've been had I chosen to be a spectator instead of a participant.
I'm pretty sure that's why God pushes us. We aren't designed to be spectators; He wants us all in.
Dare to start that conversation.
Dare to compliment even when it feels awkward.
Dare to love fiercely.
Dare to forgive and then let it go.
Dare to do that thing you feel God nudging you to do.
Dare to get off the sidelines and share who Jesus truly is.
Come on.
Grab your paddle and get in. The sun is sure to come out eventually and warm things up.
You're going to be so glad you didn't miss the adventure.

> *"For the Spirit God gave us does not make us timid, but gives us power, love and self-discipline." --2 Timothy 1:7 NIV*

Thanks, Lord, for courage—not only to experience special adventures but also to share how you have enhanced my life. You are so gracious. Amen.

Just What I Needed

The act of giving is taught, and the act of receiving is learned, but they are not necessarily in that order.

The Orange Swan Free Store was super busy yesterday, as always in December. It was especially busy this year as this was 2020, and we were in the middle of the pandemic. So many of the things we had taken for granted had changed.
Thanks to God's leading, we devised a plan to give away an entire garage full of toys. Thanks to His blessings, the weather was incredulous in making the plan work.

It's no surprise that this year has left many people with empty hearts and empty pockets. It was good to know that many shoppers found some things they needed. I always enjoy standing back and watching conversations take place between volunteers and shoppers. Connections are usually made easily. I have always wanted and prayed for the Swan to look more like a gathering of friends, the hands and feet of Christ, and different than any other resource out there.
It's been difficult through the pandemic not to pass out the hugs that usually are so automatic. It's an unnatural response to hear a person's story and not be able to embrace them. Many times, we've gone ahead, like a knee-jerk reaction. Not sorry.

Yesterday's first hour brought in a sweet memory as I connected with a friend and co-worker from the past. With a heart bigger than Texas, she has ten kids now through adoption. She loves deeply and the greatest thing about that is ten more little people will learn to love the same way. It's been shared. It's been modeled. What blessed children.

THE COLLECTION

Yesterday's last hour brought my second highlight of the day. A mom and three young children came to do their Christmas shopping. Their excitement in finding things for others was fulfilling to my slightly empty heart, which was also feeling the effects of this year.
I mentioned to the mom, " Toys are available over on the church lawn for the kids." I will not soon forget her response.
"Thanks, but today, we're focusing on picking gifts to share with others."

Kudos to this young mom. We come into this world helpless, and if blessed, we spend the majority of our first years receiving. It's right. It's necessary. But it's also necessary for us to witness and be taught the act of giving. It completes the circle.

I witnessed a lot of that yesterday. Knowing the process it takes to have a day like yesterday starts with the giving of donations. It includes all the hours the ladies give to sort the items and the hours it takes to place, arrange, and organize them. Add to that the hours praying over the heart of our mission and the time spent distributing those gifts.
We, in turn, receive smiles, thank-yous, and full hearts.

It is a complete circle paralleling the greatest gift ever.
Jesus gave up heaven to come to earth as a helpless baby. He gave up HIs life in order that we might receive life.
He gave and passed it along to us.
We received.
Now, it's our turn to model that love and example to others, to give time, service, and commitment out of gratitude for what we received.

A complete God-ordained perfect circle.

Giving is taught, receiving is learned, and God is in the midst of it all.

Thanks to those young moms for that reminder.

This is the true meaning of Christmas from the Orange Swan Free Store.

"and she gave birth to her firstborn, a son. She wrapped him in cloths and placed him in a manger, because there was no guest room available for them." --Luke 2:7 NIV

Lord, what a joy this free store ministry has been in sharing tangible things, but more importantly, sharing you. Thank you for blessing that ministry. Amen.

What a Difference Thirty-three Years Made

A few evenings ago, I walked out of the restrooms at a local mall and was met with an eerily quiet.
I closed my eyes.
I stood for a moment, and my memories transported me back 20 years. As I walked into the courtyard, I paused before moving into the line of moving people. There were no empty seats left in the Food Court. Shoppers recklessly bumped into each other as they moved quickly to their destinations. Hallways were filled with Kiosks of different vendors, and every storefront touted their sales. Christmas music was playing, and joy was in the air.

What a difference twenty years makes.

It was no different for me this morning.
As I finished the last episode of my video devotional, The Christmas Experience, I relished the picture I envisioned of the beautiful baby Jesus. Within all the feels of a soft, vulnerable baby, I was filled with the knowledge of all He had come to accomplish.
After finishing my study, I began preparing for the next 16 hours. I started listening to a daily podcast favorite; I loved listening to a woman who reads through the four gospels monthly.
Today, we picked up reading where Jesus was before the Sanhedrin in Matthew 27.
Moments before, he had been a babe in my study, swaddled in a manger. A thrill of hope, the weary world rejoiced.
And now?
And now they spat in his face and struck him with their fists.

They thrust a crown of thorns on his head, beat him, and led him away to be crucified.
What a difference 33 years had made.
How quickly things change.
A bustling mall turned ghost town.
A helpless babe turned vulnerable and beaten.
Hardly two things to compare, but I'm so glad His story didn't end there.

There may be no hope for the malls of America.
But for Jesus and because of Jesus? There was and is more than hope.
That hope is still alive today.
He was buried in the tomb after his inhumane crucifixion.
Death could not hold him in the ground.
He conquered it.
Nothing else will ever be the same.

Malls closing.
A world fighting.
Cancer.
Ongoing financial struggle.
A child with a chronic illness.
Broken marriages.
Whatever the battle,
Jesus fought.
Jesus won.
What a difference 33 years made.
What a difference His life made.

> *"Surely he took up our pain and bore our suffering, yet we considered him punished by God, stricken by him, and afflicted. But he was pierced for our transgressions, he was crushed for our iniquities; the punishment that brought us peace was on him, and by his wounds we are healed. We all, like sheep, have gone astray, each of us has turned to our own way; and the Lord has laid on him the iniquity of us all." --Isaiah 53:4-6 NIV*

Lord, Thank you for leaving the grandeur of heaven to come to earth, to live as one of us, and to die for all of us. I pray my life acknowledges the sacrifice you made for me.
Amen.

Be A Beverly

It was May, 1980.
I was summoned to the pay phone in the hallway at the Neosho County Community College dorms in Chanute, Kansas.
Yes, a huge phone was attached to the wall in a small alcove, and the college was NCCJC then.
The caller was my aunt.
After small talk, she presented the reason for the call.
"How would you like to work for me this summer at Bethesda Nursing Home?"
I knew she was the director of nursing there, but I knew nothing about caring for older people.
I had recently been accepted at Colby Junior College in their veterinary technician program. I liked caring for animals, not people.
Living in town and holding down multiple jobs appealed to me. I could stock away money for the upcoming fall semester.
I accepted her offer, not only for employment but also for a place to live. The summer began.
I fell in love. Yes, a young man was involved, but the long-lasting love was for the sweet, fragile residents.
The charm, the stories, the vulnerability, and the need for someone to help improve their daily lives were addictive.
I changed my mind. No longer was I drawn to nurturing animals, but now people. They were people living in their last days, needing someone to help make every day a better day.
Fast forward through 40 years of other varied nursing jobs, raising a family, careers that had nothing to do with nursing, losing a mom to Alzheimer's, and helping care for a father after a catastrophic hip fracture, and here I am.

Now, another aunt, my mom's sister, entered the realm of needing someone to ensure every day is better. After a stroke that changed life as she knew it, we had struggled for two months to get her moved closer to home and relatives.

Thursday, I walked through the same doors of the nursing home again, where nurturing people had become my passion.

The halls echoed memories of my young 18-year-old life. Rooms brought to mind residents' names that I have never forgotten. The former door to my aunt's office reminded me of her dedication to her job, her way of loving the residents, and how I have aspired to be just like her. She recognized that every resident had a history, a story, a family, a purpose, and a right to be treated with respect and dignity.

Rosilee doesn't work there anymore.

Beverly does. She has picked up the baton and is running her leg of the race most profoundly. She's not the director of nursing but the social service designer and admissions liaison.

It's only fitting that her office is at the front door. She is the first smile, loving embrace, and authentic heart that a new resident sees. She was the first glimpse of hope I have had on this long journey in over two months.

It takes a special person to be a Rosilee or a Beverly.

May we all aspire to treat human beings the way they do.

May we never take them for granted.

Thanks to both of them for the reminders of what life is all about.

"Do nothing out of selfish ambition or vain conceit. Rather, in humility value others above yourselves, not looking to your own interests but each of you to the interests of the others." --Philippians 2:3-4 NIV

God, Thank you for Beverlys, and Rosilees, Anna Beths, and Morgans. Thank you for people that lead with kindness and remind the rest of us why we are here. Amen.

CHAPTER 10

Let's Get Real

This chapter gives off a mysterious vibe. What exactly does "let's get real" mean? It's taken me 63 years to figure some of it out. There are still multiple areas that I am still working on.
Getting real can mean letting go of the facade and letting the world in.
It can be dropping your expectations of unrealistic things.
It can be embracing the authenticity of a child who speaks innocently.
It can be admitting you don't have all the answers, but you know the one who does.

This chapter is just a collection of stories that evoke vulnerability and honesty. They place us all on a level field–the foot of the cross. There, we learn the mystery of getting along with each other and letting Christ rule.

Coffee and Dad

There are sacred moments in a cup of coffee.
I left Dad's house this morning with my travel mug full of my favorite—black coffee.
Headed to work nearly an hour away, I drove in the dark, misty rain and conversed with my Father.
I had enjoyed a short conversation with my Dad before I left his house. Some things never change but take on a different form.
I left him in his lift chair this morning after helping him move from bed. Everything he would need was tucked neatly on a bedside table, including his phone, before my sister-in-law would arrive.
As I walked out the door, memories of a morning in December 42 years ago flooded my mind. Working in healthcare as a CNA, I always left the house by six to get to work on time. That particular morning, Dad was up. That was very unusual as he typically slept until 7:30.
We drank a cup of coffee together.
The night before, I had a date with a former boyfriend and had thought we would be getting back together. Dad had got up to see how things went. Instead of what I had hoped, the boy had broken it off. I was confused, hurt, and had lots of questions.
I remember Dad saying, "This was probably for the best anyway."
I found comfort in his words.
Now, I know there was wisdom as well.

Coffee with Dad started many years before that.
When I was younger, he began a habit at the breakfast table. As soon as breakfast was over, Dad would break out the sandwich cookies. I would pour a half cup of coffee, and the fun began. We would dip our cookies in the steaming dark liquid. The secret was to leave them long enough to make the cookie soft but not soggy.

I learned the love of coffee then—black coffee.

Our conversations then were about something other than boyfriends or whether broken hips would heal as they should.

It was math problems. Dad loved math. He still does. He loved doing problems in his head and would drill us with the same.

He was a whiz at it. He still is but cannot spell shirt, let alone pronounce it. My mom, on the other hand, was the speller, balancing out the perfect couple.

Years later, as I stayed at the house and nursed Mon through her last days, Dad and I would eat breakfast together and share a cup of coffee. The conversations were more serious then but unforgettable.

My best cups of coffee, though, have been with my Heavenly Father. Early mornings, His word speaks to me as my prayers converse with him, growing closer and wiser.

Morning after morning—

My years have contained a lot of miles, a lot of conversations, and a lot of coffee.

There are sacred moments in a cup of coffee.

> *"Very early in the morning, while it was still dark, Jesus got up, left the house and went off to a solitary place, where he prayed." --Mark 1:35 NIV*

Lord, Thank you for sacred moments with you and my earthly father. I treasure all of them. Amen.

Our Victor is Coming!

I will never forget the morning.

As I started my journey that day, I barely got into the car when it began. It was just a light rain when I started, but it wasn't too long before it turned into a monsoon.

I had to pull over a couple of times, and hail mixed into the downpour several times. Aborting the journey wasn't an option, as others depended on me.

I remember praying more fervently that day, not only for my safe passage and arrival but also for everything heavy on my heart. Desperation has a way of making us truly seek the one who is in charge of our journey.

A mile from turning onto the shortcut I usually take, the rain stopped, and the clouds started to part.

As I turned south and traveled about a mile, my eyes took in this view.

I stopped the car, took several pictures, and sat in awe momentarily.

How encouraging it would have been to know this was on the other side of the storm. All the time, I was struggling to see and fearful of what was ahead. This was waiting.

The disciples also experienced a far worse storm than the storm I had gone through. They had watched Jesus get beaten, bruised, and take his last breath on the cross. It had been nothing but turmoil, confusion, and heartbreak after he had so lovingly washed their feet. If they had stopped and remembered what he had said and trusted in His words, they would've realized that the tomb would soon be empty. They would've remembered that he said he would rise again and that everything, no matter how bad it looked, would eventually be okay.
So here's to our chaos and tragedy: the illness without a name, the news of the car wreck, the cancer diagnosis, the onset of Alzheimer's, the overdue statement from the bank, and the tragedy lurking behind the shadows.
This. Isn't. All there is.
He defeated it.

> *"Where, O death, is your victory? Where, O death,*
> *is your sting?" But thanks be to God! He gives us*
> *the victory through our Lord Jesus Christ."*
> *--1 Corinthians 1555, 57 NIV*

Our Victor is coming! Our king is coming back to get us.
And no matter how bad it looks, it's going to be okay.
He **will** make all things new!

Lord, Whether we are in the valley or on the mountaintop, we know with assurance that our final destination will be with you. Thank you for traveling with us and leading the way. Amen.

Camp Kane

My schedule landed in a way that allowed some extra family time during a hot July summer.

Camp Kane officially opened up to several grandchildren campers with a full line-up of planned activities.

This morning, after feeding our physical bodies, we also sat down to fill our spiritual ones.

I decided to try something different. I allowed each child to tell me their favorite Bible story. Then, I selected one we would talk about.

The first choice given by a grandchild involved overturning the tables in the temple. This was an interesting choice. Was there repressed anger that wanted to be righteously expressed?

Next on the list was David and Goliath. Again, this is interesting coming from a sibling sitting in the middle of their brothers and sisters.

Lastly, one grandchild picked Moses, coming down from the mountain with the Ten Commandments, seeing the golden calf, and angrily breaking the tablets.

I sensed a trend.

I decided to go with Moses, the Ten Commandments, and the whole dysfunctional group of wandering Israelites in the desert. We traced the roots back to the very beginning and how the Israelites ended up in their situation. Then we began to talk about the fact that this was a fascinating history from our Christian heritage, but what can we learn from it today? How does this look right now compared to where we are as Americans?

I fully expected to bring the lesson.

I sat back and listened. One by one, my grandchildren prodigies listed these things.

1. Stop complaining about everything.
2. Be more grateful. When we're thankful, you will have more joy.
3. Obey because God makes rules to keep us safe. Ultimately, the punishment for sin is death without Jesus.
4. God has promises for us. He will deliver on those promises if you listen to and follow Him.

The last thing this grandma learned was that sometimes you will learn more if you just hush and listen.

> *"My son, do not let wisdom and understanding out of your sight, preserve sound judgment and discretion; they will be life for you, an ornament to grace your neck." --Proverbs 3:21-22 NIV*

Lord, What a blessing I have received from the gift of my grandchildren. Thank you for entrusting them to our family. Amen.

The God Shed

Thanksgiving fell on the last day of November that year. I woke up in the middle of December like a deer looking straight into headlights. With only five days until the first of our celebrations, I ran into the Dollar Store for more wrapping paper. I hadn't expected a crowded store in the middle of a snowstorm.

In the midst of my shopping trip, I ran into a friend of mine and her little boy. Several times, I heard him excitedly showing his mom an item they needed. His expert advice on the shopping trip brought back some fond memories.

I continued to shop, and when almost done, I overheard him an aisle over. "Mom, we need that God shed."

Without looking, I knew exactly what he was talking about. It had to be the nativity. I giggled to myself. He was young, he was a farm boy, but most of all, he was innocent—a God shed.

Through the conversation, it appeared that he "needed" the nativity to share it with his brother—something about adding it to his collection.

I love the simple, uncluttered view he had of the manger scene.

We need it.

It's necessary.

It's meant to be shared.

I have nothing against Christmas movies on TV, but I have everything against them. They are all about love. They did get that right, but unfortunately, the majority of them forget to include the One who is love and the One who brought love.

I only wish my view of the nativity was that simple and that I shared his urgency to share the God shed. Thanks, Caleb.

"Today in the town of David a Savior has been born to you; he is the Messiah, the Lord. This will be a sign to you: You will find a baby wrapped in cloths and lying in a manger." --Luke 2:11-12 NIV

Lord, Thank you for the innocence of a little boy to remind us how much we need the nativity in our Christmas and in our everyday lives. Amen.

Handing Out Starbucks

It hit me today.
I finally know what I want to be when I grow up.
I'm going with the positive that there is still time for me to do that and that I WILL grow up.
Today was one of my six trips to work for the week. That's a story for another time; nonetheless, the drive is excellent prayer time. Sometimes, though, I find myself a bit exhausted before I ever arrive. Unusual with my routine, I decided to swing by Starbucks and get my daughter and me a magical brew before starting the day.
That's when it occurred!
"Good morning, Rhonda! Wow, you look great today. We've got your order coming right up. Did you get a look at that sky? We're going to have sunshine today. It's going to be beautiful.
Here's your order. I hope you enjoy it. It's going to be a great day, and by the way, your hair is just beautiful."
I didn't know whether to laugh, cry, or look in the mirror.
What a difference her infusion of positivity made in my day.
I want to work at Starbucks!
No.
Although, that's not a bad idea. (Will work for coffee.) I only want to light up people's day like she lit mine.
Three, no, two minutes, and she turned my day around. All it took was pouring a tiny bit of kindness into my heart (and some coffee in my cup.)
If we all aspire to be as kind as the woman in the Starbucks drive-thru, this world would be a much nicer place.
Tomorrow…I'm handing out Starbucks.

"Therefore encourage one another and build each other up, just as in fact you are doing." --1 Thessalonians 5:11 NIV

God, thank you for coffee and the people who make this world a brighter place. Please help me encourage at least one person on my path every day. Amen.

The Most Important One

Forty-seven years later.
I was sixteen. Short of babysitting five kids at the age of thirteen for a whole 25 cents an hour, this was my big break. This was my first real job.

The pay? A crisp ten-dollar bill! I don't remember how long it took each week or even cared.

Strip the bedding off five beds, remake them, and clean the bedrooms.
Vacuum and dust the entire house, including the vast staircase.
Mop the kitchen floor and clean the three bathrooms.
Straighten the game room.
And the best part?
Drag the vacuum up the stairs to the watchtower and vacuum the small room.

It was my understanding the family used it as a prayer room. I would linger there, gazing out the window, watching for my husband to come home from war.

It was the farthest I ever ventured from the reality of my perfect job. At sixteen, I already loved older homes and architecture, and this one did not disappoint.

Why would a sixteen-year-old girl love scrubbing someone else's home? It was hard work. Sometimes it was dirty work.

Responsibility.

Independence.

Satisfaction of standing back and seeing the transformation take place. Gratitude from my employer.

I took pride in my work and made sure the person who paid me was happy with my work.

I look back on those days lovingly and longingly. What joy to see myself emerge, to watch what my parents had instilled in me grow and come to fruition.

It was even better to watch that transformation take place in my kids.

Teaching your kids to work is invaluable. It is one of the greatest things you can do for them, next to introducing them to Jesus.

Teach them to take pride in what they do.

Details matter.

Work hard for your employer so they know you value them, and in turn, they will value you.

Hard work does not earn us righteousness but shapes our character and prepares our stamina for days ahead that might not be easy.

Ultimately, it is a reminder of Colossians 3:23:

"Whatever you do, work at it with all your heart, as working for the Lord, not for men."

Oh, to return to that home one more time.

However, now, I'd like to sit on the front porch and enjoy a good cup of coffee.

Someone else can drag that vacuum up those stairs. 😊

> *"Love the Lord your God with all your heart and with all your soul and with all your strength. These commandments that I give you today are to be on your hearts. Impress them on your children. Talk about them when you sit at home and when you walk along the road, when you lie down and when you get up."*
> *--Deuteronomy 6:5-7 NIV*

Graduation Consolation

Many events happen that will leave an impression on us for the rest of our lives. This particular one, I will never forget.

We attended my daughter's graduation. It was at a Christian college. Two years ago, one of their classmates was killed in a car wreck coming home from a ministry-related event.

Not far into the celebration, the president stopped and honored the fallen student. The student's picture was displayed on the screen as he described the young man's character, sense of humor, and boisterous personality. He made clear the impact this student had on his classmates and the hole left in so many people's hearts at his passing. He then asked the crowd to show their love to the attending family that day.

The crowd began to clap, and after three to four minutes, one by one, everyone stood. The ovation and clapping continued, putting a lump in my throat. The family sat surrounded by an auditorium of people, showing them reverence, respect, compassion, sympathy, and love for a still-hurting family. Most of all, it was conveyed that they did not carry their grief alone. They were surrounded by people who cared. People who would not want to trade places with them for anything but would walk beside and help carry their burden.

People who wanted them to know, "Your child has not been forgotten."

Nothing about this display of love for this family took away from the graduates' celebration. It added to it, as the clapping surely had to echo to heaven. Everyone there knew where their son and friend eternally resided.

Graduation is a celebration, but it's also a student send-off to enter the world—a world that is not all about your happiness, celebrations, or you all the time. It's about life and how we can get through it together.

There's been so much in the past few years that moves us more and more towards self-centeredness. This is not the way God intended for us to live.

Life is real and messy; it can hurt and tear you apart. We were put here to carry each other's burdens. And if that means giving up five minutes of your day of celebration to honor and love a family that doesn't get to celebrate that day, then I think it's worth the five minutes.

That's what real life is all about.

"Above all, love each other deeply, because love covers over a multitude of sins. Offer hospitality to one another without grumbling. Each of you should use whatever gift you have received to serve others, as faithful stewards of God's grace in its various forms." 1 Peter 4:8-10 NIV

Jesus, I don't know how we would get through the dark valleys without you and those around us. Help us to always be aware of who might need extra love. Thank you for an abundant supply. Amen.

The Woman at the Grocery Store

I pulled into the parking lot and shut off the car. I scanned my surroundings, not recognizing any reason I might want to avoid the store today. I proceeded to go in.

I soon realized I had missed a clue. There, in aisle two, right next to the spaghetti sauce, was a former close friend.

Not today.

I was still reeling from an earlier phone call. Another "friend" who felt the need to share the latest gossip about me had phoned. I couldn't face another person who was disappointed in me.

I darted to the crushed tomatoes, picked up the wrong-sized can, threw it in my cart, and moved on. My friend pretended not to see me and never looked up.

I continued my "dodge and dart" until I had picked up everything on my list. My furtive glances continued until I was safely out the door and inside my car. I sighed heavily. I was tired.

With my marriage ending and my divorce almost final, I didn't feel very welcome in most places I went. Everyone had their own version of my story. Have you ever been in on one of those? You know, the rumor mill? Honestly, I've been there. I have been the one on the other side sharing a story I only knew because someone had told their friend, who in turn told my friend who then told me.

Yes, my story was all the things TV soap operas were made of. There was messiness here.

Plain truth.

I had played a great part in destroying my marriage.

No one knew the whole complete truth... except One. And quite honestly, I had been avoiding him as well.

Step back with me for a moment.

Picture the Samaritan woman at the well. Remember her? The thirsty one? The one who had five husbands and was living with the sixth prospect. Spoiler alert here.
She left her jar of water and ran back into town to tell them about Jesus. This was the woman who had gone to the well in the heat of the day to avoid the other women—the woman who had chosen isolation due to the mess she had made of her life.
"Come see a man who told me everything I ever did. Could this be the Messiah!"
All of this because Jesus happened to be there at the well?
At the same time?
Coincidence? Hardly.

The passage is found in John 4.

> *"Eventually he came to the Samaritan village of Sychar, near the field that Jacob gave to his son Joseph. Jacob's well was there; and Jesus, tired from the long walk, sat wearily beside the well about noontime.*

The woman was surprised, for Jews refuse to have anything to do with Samaritans. She said to Jesus, *"You are a Jew, and I am a Samaritan woman. Why are you asking me for a drink?"* Jesus replied, *"If you only knew the gift God has for you and who you are speaking to, you would ask me, and I would give you living water."*

> *Jesus replied, "Anyone who drinks this water will soon become thirsty again. But those who drink the water I give will never be thirsty again. It becomes a fresh, bubbling spring within them, giving them eternal life."*
> *--John 4:5-7, 9-10, 13-14 NLT*

Their conversation quickly changed from Jesus asking for water to explaining about living water. But then, Jesus started to reveal that he knew more about this woman than she knew about herself.

> *"Please, sir,"* the woman said, *"give me this water! Then I'll never be thirsty again, and I won't have to come here to get water."* "Go

and get your husband," Jesus told her. "I don't have a husband," the woman replied. Jesus said, "You're right! You don't have a husband— for you have had five husbands, and you aren't even married to the man you're living with now. You certainly spoke the truth!"
--John 4:15-18 NLT

Realizing she was talking to more than just a man she began to question one of the great debates between the Jews and Samaritans, where to worship. Whether this was her attempt to keep from having to look Jesus directly in the eye or the beginning of a real thirst, I'm not sure.

"But the time is coming—indeed it's here now—when true worshipers will worship the Father in spirit and in truth. The Father is looking for those who will worship him that way. For God is Spirit, so those who worship him must worship in spirit and in truth." (The debate was answered. It didn't matter where you worship but how.) The woman said, "I know the Messiah is coming—the one who is called Christ. When he comes, he will explain everything to us." Then Jesus told her, "I AM the Messiah!"
--John 4:23-26 NLT

And thus, one confrontation, one conversation and her shame began to fade. Her hiding was over. She had bigger things to share than the sorrow of her own failings. All of a sudden it wasn't about her. It was about hope. It was about sharing that hope.
 No matter who she was.
No matter what she'd done.
This was far more important!
And so she left her jar of water and ran back into town.

My transformation took longer. Maybe I was able to avoid that eye contact longer.
Maybe I had avoided His presence in a fashion just like that day at the grocery store.
One thing is for sure. He pursued me, just like the woman at the well.
He invited me despite the mess I had made of my life.
He told me I was worth saving, even when others threw me away.

Despite whatever was in my rearview mirror, He told me there was hope ahead of me.
Here I am.
The one who once sought isolation because of my shame proudly proclaims, "Come and see! I know a Man who knew everything about me but loved me anyway. This is the Messiah!"

I can never repay you for your love, your kindness, your forgiveness. Jesus, thank you for loving me like no one else. Amen.

The First Three

Three months finally transitioned into four. I drew in a deep breath and decided I could let my guard down.
After all, the doctor had said that the first three months were the most dangerous time in a pregnancy. A few short weeks later, I began to feel the gentle flutter of life within me. As soon as I get the sonogram done, I will relax and let my guard down, I thought.
The sonogram went well, but the next few months were filled with concern. Some days, the baby didn't kick as much; other days, she never stopped.
I knew I could stop worrying as soon as I gave birth. I could hold this baby and know that everything was okay.
A month later, the doctor delivered a beautiful baby by way of cesarean section, and I drew in a deep breath. Life could begin now, and I would put my worries aside.
The first year was filled with some of the happiest days of my life, but even so, she was so fragile that I just couldn't let my guard down. The preschool years went quickly and were filled with earaches, strep throat, and stomach viruses. I tried to trust God but clung to that little corner of worry as if it were mine.
Starting school brought new concerns, friends, grades, injuries, and sports. And then a new worry presented itself: boys. I never dreamt how much concern this would cause me.
She made her way off to college, and it was as if a grown woman was hiding in my womb again. I could sense her struggles and growing pains, but she was out of sight and literally out of state. So, I worried even more that she was okay.
I knew I would relax as soon as this chapter ended.
The day came, and that chapter closed, but a new one began.
She was presented with an engagement ring.

Time flew, plans and decorations materialized, and I knew it was time to hand my worries over to someone else.

As she drove off into the horizon with her new mate, I took a deep breath, excited for this journey to begin.

Somehow, I didn't get to hand my worries over to her new mate; instead, I added him to my list of people to worry about.

About a year in, I got the excited text that the test had returned positive. The first three months are so vulnerable.

I can take a deep breath when we get past the first three.

The above story unfolds like a one-act play. Even the least curious readers would wonder if this story was true. Similar would be a better way to describe it.

I have spent a lifetime shadowboxing the "what-ifs." They lurk in the shadows of every season of life and can consume us if we allow them.

It has been said that the Bible states 365 times, "Do not be afraid." Some sources say that is false. I don't have an exact answer, but I have enough scriptures memorized on fear, trust, and peace to know that Jesus is serious about trusting in Him.

I've often wondered why I struggle with having control over so many things I have no control over.

It will always be a daily decision.

Do I carry a burden that I have no control over, or do I hand it to the One in control? The simplest answer will always be the hardest.

> *"So do not fear, for I am with you; do not be dismayed, for I am your God. I will strengthen you and help you; I will uphold you with my righteous right hand. --Isaiah 41:10 NIV*
>
> *"I sought the Lord, and he answered me; he delivered me from all my fears."*
> *--Psalms 344 NIV*

Lord, I confess my anxiety, fear, and lack of faith. I long to have faith in you completely. Thank you for always being patient with me. Amen.

What Exactly Is Normal?

Putting the finishing touches on a book is never easy. It has taken years to write and months to edit. Editing can be a marathon task, but my schedule doesn't allow marathons; I only do sprints.

In the past four months, included in my normal day-to-day life, I have endured the loss of my niece's infant, the loss of an uncle, became the guardian of my aunt, and encountered another hospitalization for my father. In addition, two of my kids are dealing with health issues. In the past month, I totaled my favorite car from a massive deer, was hit again by a deer in my new vehicle twenty days later, and had to put our golden retriever down. She had been our best friend for 18 years. Last night, I had another scare that Dad might be going to the hospital again.

My husband was working the night shift, so the house was quiet. I was alone.

Almost in tears, I yelled out, "I want normal!"

As I sat there listening to the empty silence, I realized I did have normal. Not only did I have normal, I was living on the blessed side of it.

A while back, I purchased my first scripture mapping book. I was unfamiliar with this practice until I caught an ad and was intrigued. This particular book gives multiple ways to dissect a straightforward verse, read it in different versions, reflect on how God meant it, reflect on how to apply it and end with a prayer to seal the deal.

After the second car accident, I came home and stared at the wall. For some reason, I walked over to my Scripture Mapping book, picked it up and began to finish a scripture I had started earlier. Rather than one verse, it was a section of scripture:

> *"Love the Lord your God with all your heart and with all your soul and with all your strength. These commandments that I give you*

today are to be on your hearts. Impress them on your children. Talk about them when you sit at home and when you walk along the road, when you lie down and when you get up. Tie them as symbols on your hands and bind them on your foreheads. Write them on the doorframes of your houses and on your gates." --Deuteronomy 6:5-9 NIV

After going through the first steps of the mapping, I came to the Reflection and Application section.

I wrote:

I totaled my car from a deer twenty days ago. Today, a deer ran into the side of my new car. What does this have to do with this verse?

Everything. It's how we live in the good times. It's how we live in the bad. The world, also known as family, friends, and co-workers, is watching our reaction to how we handle life. If we have placed enough reminders in place, we will remember what it means to love him with all your heart. It will be reflected in our speech, our actions, reactions, and how we treat others. It will be evident in how we handle **adversity.**

And guess who is watching all of this? The very ones we were called to impress this upon. Our kids. Our grandkids. And I think that includes our friends and co-workers.

We are being watched. A page-long list of praises has accompanied my events in the past months. He has been present and evident in every one of these tragedies. That's the part I want my world to know about. Normal life consists of ups and downs, good times and hardships. That's what normal is. How we act or react will make the most significant impact on his Kingdom.

That is the reason I keep writing my thoughts and impressions down. It's a reminder to me. I hope it's a reminder to you.

He is always there, helping us through our normal, whatever that may be. Always.

Lord, give me the endurance to continue to rise early to study your word and seek your leading. Give me reminders on how quickly we can tarnish our reputation. Remind me how we damage our witness when we don't keep your guidance in front of us, and make mistakes that others find misleading.

Notes

Mercy
1. https://dictionary.cambridge.org/us/dictionary/english/reject
2. **"Graves into Gardens Lyrics."** *Lyrics.com.* STANDS4 LLC, 2024. Web. 2 Jul 2024. <https://www.lyrics.com/lyric/37053561/Elevation+Worship/Graves+into+Gardens>.
3. **The Worship Initiative - Abide Lyrics** | AZLyrics.com Container: www.azlyrics.com URL: https://www.azlyrics.com/lyrics/shaneshane/abide.htm

Jesus
1. **"Only You Lyrics."** *Lyrics.com.* STANDS4 LLC, 2024. Web. 2 Jul 2024. <https://www.lyrics.com/lyric/6533134/David+Crowder/Only+You>.

Be Intentional
1. **"In Jesus Name (God Of Possible) Lyrics."** *Lyrics.com.* STANDS4 LLC, 2024. Web. 2 Jul 2024.<https://www.lyrics.com/lyric-lf/7653300/Katy+Nichole/In+Jesus+Name+%28God+Of+Possible%29>.

Trust
1. **"Graves into Gardens Lyrics."** *Lyrics.com.* STANDS4 LLC, 2024. Web. 2 Jul 2024. <https://www.lyrics.com/lyric/37053561/Elevation+Worship/Graves+into+Gardens>.

Scripture quotations marked (NLT) are taken from the Holy Bible, New Living Translation, copyright 1996, 2004, 2015 by Tyndale House Foundation. Used by permission of Tyndale House Publishers, a Division of Tyndale House Ministries, Carol Stream, Illinois 60188. All rights reserved.

Scripture quotations marked (NIV) are taken from the Holy Bible, New International Version, NIV. Copyright 1973, 1978, 1984, 2011 by Biblica, Inc. Used by permission of Zondervan. All rights reserved worldwide. www.zondervan.com The "NIV" and "New Internation Version" are trademarks registered in the United States Patent and Trademark Office by Biblica, Inc.

Scripture quotations marked CSB have been taken from the Christian Standard Bible, Copyright 2017 by Holman Bible Publishers. Used by permission. Christian Standard Bible and CSB are federally registered trademarks of Holman Bible Publishers.

Scripture quotations marked MSG are taken from THE MESSAGE, copyright 1993, 2002, 2018 by Eugene H. Peterson. Used by permission of NavPress. All rights reserved. Represented by Tyndale House Publishers, a Division of Tyndale House Ministries.

Scripture quotations marked (KJV) are taken from the King James Versionof the Bible.

Closing Reflections

I sat in my back room and scanned through the manuscript. I pried it from my hands, prayed for God to continue his work, and dropped it into the Google link—a four-year compilation of my heart inspired by the Holy Spirit. The publisher would have it soon.

My emotions range from elated, scared, vulnerable, and hopeful. I want, more than anything, for people to know Jesus intimately.

Last week, multiple boxes of quilting items came into the free store. Patterns drawn out for future projects, fabric purchased and separated into ziplock bags, squares cut, and the appropriate thread selected revealed future plans. Unfortunately, the quilter passed before finishing the projects. It struck me as prophetic.

I love quilts and the idea of how they come about. I would love to see that hobby in my future, but I have said many times that I do not have the patience to work on a project for that length of time.

Quilts tell a story. They may center around fabrics that have belonged to different family members, t-shirts from a child's school memories, designs that share a message, or family lineage. Each stitch combines to tell a story.

This current project has taken me four years. It appears I have more patience than I knew. Each word, combined with emotion and memories, tells a story. Some are of family members, childhood lessons, regretful moments, and people who have inspired my life. They are pieces of art, revealing a beautiful picture, and within that picture, God is always present.

I hope this collection blesses people's lives and leads them to moments of finding God right where they are.

www.ingramcontent.com/pod-product-compliance
Lightning Source LLC
LaVergne TN
LVHW010157070526
838199LV00062B/4395